What d

have to do to get a book published!

The essential guide to self-publishing for the UK market

Jo Anthony

First published in Great Britain by
Pen Press Publishers Ltd
39-41, North Road
Islington
London N7 9DP

ISBN 1-905203-58-6

Printed and bound in the UK

A catalogue record of this book is available from
the British Library

www.indepublishing.com

Self-publishing has arrived as a viable and credible route to market. There are many who are fiercely resisting it and some in the publishing and bookselling industry who denounce it, but they are gradually becoming small and lonely voices.

It has proved a successful route for many, and will continue to do so as independent authors produce better and better quality material. This is the key, and this book is designed to show you what that means and how you can go about achieving that.

CONTENTS

INTRODUCTION

The publishing industry has been teetering on the edge of change for the last ten years – since the abolition of the Net Book Agreement (NBA), the growth of Amazon and heavy discounting by supermarkets. Yet despite external changes, the business of publishing is fiercely resistant to change. When you peer inside a publishing house, you will discover the ghosts of Edwardian publishing – unnecessary bureaucracy over the protection or sale of rights, contracts in age-old legalese and print order forms that still refer to pre-digital technologies ie. camera-ready films. It is time to look to tomorrow, to see where publishing is going and openly to embrace the change – the impact of technologies and the recognition that self-publishing is a credible route to the market.

During the 1990s, the photographic world suddenly realised that digital technology and image manipulation seriously threatened the management of copyright over images. It was a case of either Adapt or Die. Image libraries got their act together and created online libraries where sale of copyrighted material was made easy. Today, photographers and illustrators earn more out of their image library material than they EVER did before selling to a global market.

In the last five years, the music industry nearly collapsed under the demands and pressures from the public for the music corporations to loosen their strangle-hold on the music business. They resisted, but the winds of change were blowing and, despite dubious legal defences, Napster kept winning court cases, ultimately changing the way the music industry works. And now, for the first time ever, you will find new little indie bands at number 65 in the charts, sitting alongside established classics like U2 or the compiled sound of Ibiza this summer. What we are seeing is an emerging meritocracy, rather than the charts being controlled by whoever spent the biggest promotional budget.

The publishing industry has been fiercely resisting the changes that emerging technologies bring. Certainly, these changes bring new headaches and problems to solve – digital rights management, ease of using copyrighted material without permissions; not to mention the flood of new titles hitting the market.

This 'flood' is one of the biggest criticisms about self-publishing. Many complain that the ease of self-publishing has resulted in a glut of books on the market, many of which are low quality – even pure rubbish. Many others argue that enough rubbish titles are produced by the mainstream publishers.

These are definitely complex problems, but the drumbeat of advancing change is getting louder and louder – time marches on and waits for no man.

Five years ago I tried to publish a book that I had personally looked for and not found a year earlier, but there was nothing on the shelves at the time. I had just survived a year of treatment for breast cancer at the young age of 35, and I had written my account of that year when I was shuffled from operating theatre through chemotherapy and radiotherapy to hormone therapy. I then tried to re-assemble my life back into the shape it had been before I was diagnosed, but it had irrevocably changed.

I desperately wanted to help other people who found themselves in the self-same situation. I wrote my book and approached several agents and publishers, who all assured me that there was plenty of material out there already by far more famous people than me; I was firmly rejected.

Because I had not written the book for financial gain and I had money in savings, I decided to self-publish my book, *Career, Kids and Breast Cancer* with a small company in Brighton called Pen Press. They did a sterling job on it, and I developed an interest in self-publishing that resulted in my working with them in a marketing capacity two years later.

Most of the sales of my books to date were private sales, rather than 'through the tills', which was fine for my objectives but wouldn't suit everybody. The nub of the problem was the reticence of the industry about accepting self-published titles. "They are rubbish... it's just vanity... there is no market..." was the only response.

It has been a long, slow haul for self-publishers to gain acceptance by the rest of the industry. In the course of my involvement in self-publishing, I have encountered many closed doors, met some very reluctant dinosaurs and communicated with some people are remain steadfastly anti-self-publishing. Still, I firmly believe that time has moved on; authors will look to other routes to market and self-publishing will become increasingly more credible as long as authors produce work of quality.

The real task is to help authors produce work of quality.

The purpose of this book is to help the self-publishing author to publish a title that can compete effectively in the marketplace. It does this by advising on the essential tasks that have to be undertaken, lifting the veil of some of the secrecy and myths that exist and pointing you in the direction of services and organisations that can help and provide more in-depth information than I have covered here.

What do I have to do to get a book published! seeks to present an honest and balanced view of the publishing industry, giving new perspectives to inspire positive change. The main aim is to raise the standard of self-published titles and eradicate any negatives people attach to these books.

In order to inspire change, this book seeks to give new perspectives and not trot out the same tired old beliefs and accusations, citing 'she who must not be named' as proof that publishers cannot recognise potential when they see it. Most good books get through – the rest have to find alternative routes. I agree with mainstream publishers that, if a book is good, it will get there in the end; but I would add that there may be an easier and faster route – self-publishing. In this competitive day and age, the author just has to work that much harder, but he can earn greater percentage rewards from it.

I hope you find this book informative. You can contact me via my website (www.indepublishing.com) either with your comments, to arrange a talk about self-publishing or for publishing & marketing consultancy. I look forward to hearing from you.

Jo Anthony

FOREWORD BY STEPHEN CLARKE

I still have the rejection letters for *A Year in the Merde.*

"I can't see this selling in the UK," they say. Or "Peter Mayle has cornered the market for books about France."

I'd written a pitch for the novel and a sample chapter, and wanted to test the water. The water, it turned out, was cold, as were the feet of publishers and agents.

"OK, forget it," I said, and decided to self-publish.

I wrote the novel, did the cover and blurbs, and got 200 books printed. I hawked the books around bookshops and posted the opening pages (the same sample I'd sent out to publishers and agents) on the internet. 'Let the readers decide,' I thought.

Word of mouth spread, the books began to sell, and within three months I'd sold the rights to a major publisher. A year later, thanks to the major publisher's expertise in marketing and distributing, *A Year in the Merde* had sold around 175,000 copies in the UK alone. I say this not to boast, but to motivate.

The thing is, publishers and agents can't know what will and won't sell, because literature is not a science. Sure, they know that the next Dan Brown novel will be a hit. But they have no idea who the next Dan Brown will be. And often, they don't have the budgets to take a risk.

Which is why self-publishing is so important.

You might be the next Dan Brown, or whoever, but they still might tell you, "I can't see this selling." If you self-publish, you can provide proof that it will.

I have another letter, too, from an agent… "Sorry," it says, "I was wrong."

Stephen Clarke is the author of *A Year in the Merde* and *Merde Actually* (Bantam Press).

PART I

THE PUBLISHING INDUSTRY ROUND-UP

Before embarking on publishing journey, authors would be wise to understand the lay of the land within the world of publishing and bookselling today. This chapter is intended to show you the current picture, where some complexities lay and how change is unsettling the status quo – and to raise the questions of what this means to the self-publishing author.

UNDERSTANDING THE PUBLISHING INDUSTRY

The obvious fact that hits the newcomer to the publishing industry is the sheer volume and speed of change, and the impact this change is having on the main pillars of the publishing world.

In order to exploit any opportunities within publishing, it is of paramount importance that the self-publishing author fully understands the state of the publishing industry. It is a maze of open doors and dead-ends. Like a maze, there is no guide and the information you require is scattered. The clues are hidden and you will take many wrong turns. Unlike a maze, there are many routes to success in publishing and the scenario keeps changing. The wise author plans, listens, learns and adapts.

Publishers and booksellers are slugging it out in a sea of high price discounting, copyright protections, size and scale against small independent, online/offline etc. It's a world gone crazy, and in amongst all of this – where's the author?

Where's the person that originates the manuscript? It would appear that a polarisation is taking place with some authors doing extremely well, whilst the majority struggle on – similar to the music industry, the acting industry, etc etc etc. But one trend is staring us all in the face. On a weekly basis, new "self-publishing" ventures are being launched in their many varied forms. And more authors are turning to this route in order to take control of that which they have completely lost control of – their work.

Where "vanity" publishing has always been a rude word in publishing, "self-publishing" is now a recognised and credible route to the market. Many people try to draw a distinction between vanity and self-publishing, but whether you do the whole gamut of work completely independently, or whether you enlist the services of a company, you are self-publishing. The caveat to this remains, as it always has, that authors who self-publish MUST ensure they have fully investigated their options and KNOW what they are buying into. In any industry, there exist cowboys who are not qualified to offer the services they claim to be expert at. The author must therefore thoroughly vet all claims, and avoid anyone who is either cagey with their answers or inflexible about meeting their needs.

This book is designed to inform you about what questions to ask.

The range of publishing options today

There is a wealth of information out there about how to publish a book, how to approach agents or publishers or how to file the rejection slips etc. *The Writer's Handbook* and *The Writers' & Artists' Yearbook* are two extremely helpful books with comprehensive listings, but most manuscripts get rejected.

Once you have exhausted the extensive database of contacts listed within these tomes, you then turn your attention towards self-publishing. You quickly find it is a confusing marketplace – a wealth of information, loads of it, scattered everywhere, but it is chaotic and bewildering – some call it vanity publishing, others argue that it isn't vanity; some say you should never pay to be published, others swear it is the only way to get published; the Brits shy away from it, the Americans shout about the 22,000 who published with them last year alone. A few have experienced huge success by self-publishing, others say they were ripped off. Who to believe?

Confusion upon confusion is heaped upon the individual. On the one hand, I have been expressly advised that the TLS *'only reviews books by mainstream publishers'* but on the other, many reports confirm that self-publishing is the new route to publication. And figures from Nielsen BookData confirm this claim.

Nielsen BookData have added 2,400 new first-time applicants since the beginning of 2005; this equates to 10 new publishers every working day. This is, without doubt, due to the increase in self-publishing authors and the increase of self-publishing as a viable route to market.

Since January 2005, 2,400 new publishers have been added to the Nielsen BookData database.

The common message emerging from copious research is that successfully self-published authors advise the learning curve was steep, they made a lot of mistakes and it was a hard, hard slog. From my own experience, every time I asked the industry a question I was given an answer only to find out further down the line that I was only given HALF an answer. It was as though I was being taunted – being told only a specific answer in the absence of knowing what questions to ask.

The choice of books out there is overwhelming, with 140,000 new titles released in the UK in 2004 alone and climbing. Nielsen BookData advise that the first 5 months of 2005 have resulted in a staggering 114,669 new titles added to the database already!! This is equivalent to 802 new titles daily.

Attending the London Book Fair, it is a humbling experience to see so many books out there, and you know that it is merely the tip of the iceberg. So much effort and for what return?

114,669 new titles have already been released to date in 2005

This is a rise of 11% since 2004

According to Nielsen Bookscan who publish the Bestseller charts, there is no fixed definition to the term "bestseller". There are weeks when the top selling title has sold a million units and other weeks when the top seller has sold only 12,000 units. It is a moving target, but it can be said that any book that sells approximately 110+ units per week will appear in the Top 5000 chart. This means that only 7,000 books from all categories sold in excess of 5,000 units in 2004; yet there were over 550,000 different titles sold during the year!

Given that the total number of books sold in 2004 (through the tills sales as recorded by Nielsen Bookscan) was in excess of 200 million units across all categories, we can deduce the following:

To appear in a top 5000 chart, you need to sell 110 units p/w

Only 7000 books sold more than 5000 units in 2004.

(i) that the market is very fragmented, and

(ii) that there are very few authors sell an adequate enough volume of books to earn a living from writing.

These figures won't provide the income one expects from a "bestseller". Bearing in mind that all contracts vary, let's assume a first-time author's fictional work is selling in the home market for an average price of £7.99 in paperback. The average contract returning 8% royalty on net receipts will provide the following:

Bookprice:	£7.99
Average bookseller discount:	50%
Net receipts back to publisher:	£3.99
Publisher takes 92%	£3.67
Author receives 8% net	£0.32
110 units per week, nets author	**£35.20**

110 units per week looks easy to achieve to the new author, and some do achieve it for a short period, but it is difficult.

We continue to output more books than people are prepared to buy – in the UK we produced more than 140,000 new titles last year; in the US they produced more than 175,000 new titles whilst the number of new books sold dropped by nearly 44 MILLION books! This trend is set to continue with increased re-selling of books (ie. Amazon Marketplace); and with e-books increasing in popularity, particularly in the educational and reference categories.

What choices are open to authors?

There are many, many routes to publication nowadays – some are traditional routes and some are alternative or new routes given today's technology.

Traditionally available avenues:

- Literary agents
- Mainstream / conglomerate publishers
- Small independent publishers

Alternative and new avenues:

- Self-publishing services companies inc. consultancies
- Printers / POD (Print-on-Demand)
- E-publishing
- Production-financed agreements with a mainstream publisher

But are these really choices? This implies that the author has some say in the matter, but slush piles and rejection slips confirm that this is not the case. Many authors are left, not wondering whether to sign a traditional publishing agreement or to self-finance their publication, but trying to decide what form of self-financed publishing route they should follow.

> **The only choice facing authors is what method of self-publishing he will use**

Even if the author successfully secures a deal with a mainstream publisher, would they actually promote and service that author? There are so many stories of despondent authors who, after the first excitement of securing a deal, have felt subsequently let down or out of control. Many first-time authors report a sense of having their text considerably altered and the only marketing support was to put the title through the standard paces - onto distributor and wholesaler lists, into catalogues sent to bookshops and a handful of publishing rights sold in other countries. When the book made it into a range of outlets, it was either piled on the promotional table with loads of others - discounts of which were passed to the author - or just placed spine-side out on the racks upon racks of other books.

Having made the decision to explore self-financed publication, the new author then discovers an alarming array of individuals and companies all offering a myriad of different services and all saying different things. The plot thickens, and the self-publishing author is quickly confused, and easily make the wrong decisions during his journey to publish his book.

THE CHANGING INDUSTRY

The industry is changing - and everyone is in full agreement on this fact. Sadly, this is about the only area of agreement. The changes are leaving a trail of arguments, finger-pointing and accusation between the main pillars of the industry - the author, the publisher, the distributors, the booksellers, the readers. *NB Bear in mind, this is a snapshot of today and will change again tomorrow.*

There are many small reasons for change, but the three main reasons are (i) the web (ii) developing technology (iii) heavy discounting:

(i) The impact of the worldwide web

The web is changing the marketplace for most products, and books are no exception. It changes the way books are sold and the size of the market they can potentially reach; blogs are changing the way people find books and are referred to interesting and niche titles.

The way publishers sell to booksellers has changed; the web offers a more practical and cost-effective promotional medium. Penguin is one company who have recently recognised this and eliminated the production of 6-monthly catalogues.

The value of internet sales of £40bn is equivalent to Britain's entire defence budget

"The value of the internet sales doubled last year to just under £40bn, with predictions that it will increase by 40% in 2005. This increase is across all sectors and businesses of all sizes, and is between 5-8 times faster than high street sales every year" Ashley Seager, The Guardian, 23/11/04

The internet has had a surprising impact on libraries too:

"Book borrowing fell by a further 5% last year, maintaining a 20 year trend. Yet an extra 4% of people walked through library doors in 2003-04 – a fact credited largely to internet terminals being readily available in libraries." John Ezard, The Guardian, 21/5/2005

And an impact on book clubs:

Lisa Milton, outgoing Editorial Director of BCA, this week countered claims that book club sales continue to decline in the face of increasing online sales. She advised that whilst *"book club sales are down overall in direct mail, the last five years has seen a growth of online sales of 99% volume growth. Our direct marketing delivers a service driven by customer need, met by our online service BOL.com. We can leverage their database of membership information and tailor our offer accordingly ie. we react to the fact that there is an increase of 21% of male, adult buyers (2001-04), and the high take up of pre- and post-war romantic fiction by ladies of a 'certain age'."* Publishing News 4/5/05

(ii) The impact of technology

Recent developments in technology have enabled digital printing methods to create very short runs of books, and 'print-on-demand' ie. books exist only 'virtually' until they are ordered. Within 48 hrs, a good POD printer can have a book printed and ready for despatch to any country in the world.

Digital printing certainly has its benefits. It is ideal for low-selling titles, reprinting out-of-print titles, books sold online in the international marketplace - not to mention being very ecological. It enables people to test the market with a short print run, instead of felling a rainforest to produce a book that may only sell 200 copies. Indeed, POD titles are not even printed until someone has bought it! POD has its disadvantages as we see later on but these are far outweighed by the positives.

E-publishing is another emerging area that is currently dismissed as not being a threat to the traditional publishing market, but personally I believe this is going to come quicker than the establishment suspects. And it will have a big impact when it does.

(iii) The impact of heavy discounting

Up until 1997, publishers had the legal right to set a minimum retail price for their titles under the Net Book Agreement (NBA). A powerful influence in the decision to abolish minimum retail prices was the growth of bookseller retail chains which grew the market by 30% (1996).

The benefits of the abolition of this agreement were perceived to be that booksellers would be given the freedom to launch full-scale marketing as undertaken by UK supermarkets ie. price promotions, loyalty cards and database marketing based on customer purchasing.

Between 1996 - 2001, more than one in ten independent book shops have folded.

Anti-abolitionists claimed that this would only lead to a domination of mass-market titles such as chick-lit, crime-thriller and famous people biographies, and that the main losers would be independent booksellers who would go out of business, unable to compete.

Guess what? The major chains are dominated by chick-lit, crime-thriller and famous people biographies, and we have seen many casualties in the independent bookseller market as they are unable to compete. Between 1996 and 2001, more than one in ten independent bookshops folded, and the trend has continued steadily.

The industry that historically thrived on 'handselling' should be ashamed that so many small businesses are forced to shut down. Many voices claim that 'the internet cannot replace the experience of browsing in a bookshop, yet too few people are rallying around trying to stop the demise of the small bookseller.

The battle over discounting

Today's common practice of heavy discounting is benefiting few people - arguably it is only the top, mass-market sellers that reap the rewards of selling in scale as the bookselling business becomes increasingly commoditised. Many say that the main beneficiaries are the supermarkets. Small booksellers are folding at an alarming rate and the major book chains reported a huge shortfall over block-buster releases - where they expect to make the most money. Ultimately, the publisher and author take the hit and pay the price.

"Current discounting policies have developed in a way that abolitionists of the NBA did not foresee or welcome – Amazon using price discounting to lure buyers; supermarkets offering bestsellers as loss-leaders; and chain-store booksellers competing fiercely between themselves. The point was to enable retailers to differentiate themselves, not squeeze out creative instore ranges and independent booksellers," says Julian Rivers for The Bookseller.com

"The mountain of discounted books at supermarkets isn't democratising publishing but dumbing it down. What real choice is being offered in supermarket book displays? What is democratic in selling Jamie Oliver's latest for £2 cheaper than in Waterstones?" DJ Taylor, Guardian Unltd, 24/05/05

"When authors and agents agreed to high discount provision, they did not sign up to the now commonplace principle that 75-80% of sales were made at a high discount, resulting in a royalty of four-fifths of the prevailing rate at best." A P Watt Ltd on behalf of Derek Johns

"Independents, unlike most chains, concentrate on books, not products. Since centralisation, everything is arranged by people who are experts at everything except books," says Andrew Stilwell, manager of London Review Bookshop, quoting Colin Toibin. "The key of a good bookshop is not just stocking what people expect, but second-guessing what people will be surprised and excited by – providing that fortunate encounter."

Brian Finch, Director of Maher Booksellers recently reacted to the fact that publishers strangle the independent publishing and bookselling business:

"They give the large multiples (chainstores) such big discounts that the independent sector cannot compete; they direct author signings to the chains; they supply book clubs much too soon after publication, draining business from the retail trade; they sell their marketing support to the chains; they sell direct to schools and businesses – then wonder what happened to the independent sector which is far more profitable for publishers." Publishing News 11/7/05

The stalwarts, such as the London Review Bookshop are demonstrating their protest. The latter bookshop has recently resorted to obvious sarcasm by discounting the latest Harry Potter by 1p to £16.98, and offering 2 books for the price of 3… take three books up to the till and the cashier will remove the trashiest one. It's funny and it makes a point, but it doesn't change the reality.

The real losers in this sea of heavy discounting are the small and independent publishers and booksellers. As small bookshops fold and buying & promotion becomes increasingly centralised in bookstore chains, the small publisher finds it increasingly harder to either (i) make margin on his smaller print runs or (ii) gain any kind of visibility in the high street.

The real question is how is this going to change? How are small, independents (both publishers and booksellers) going to co-ordinate themselves and protect their futures? And what does this mean to the self-publishing author?

With the domination of chain bookshops in the high street, it is increasingly harder for self-publishing authors to gain high street presence, even at a local level, and even more so at a regional or national level. As the volume of titles being produced increases, as it undoubtedly will with the ease of self-publishing, and fewer authors will gain in-store display. This won't stop a self-publishing author, who will find other routes to market and will work harder to prove his book has an audience – but it will impact on the overall industry as the high street focuses only on mass-market material, not niche titles.

The critics of publishing say

The main rumble of opinion is aimed at the large conglomerate publishing houses whose muscle power can make or break independents (booksellers, authors, small publishing houses).

One criticism is that the conglomerates focus too heavily on big names, celebrity biographies and mass-market genres; and not enough time, effort and investment is spent on nurturing quality talent. Sadly, these titles are clearly heavily demanded by the market and one can argue that the conglomerates are only fulfilling a demand. Surely this criticism is more of an indictment about the low-brow demands of our nation?

It is common practice when looking at the power of the corporation and future implications to look across the sea to America, the founding father of 'big', and the picture does not look rosy.

"It's no secret that the publishing industry has become a man-eat-man microcosm of Wall Street greed. The major publishing houses are primarily interested in big names and sure sellers that'll pull in

big bucks. Quality content has fallen to the wayside, becoming more an added bonus than a priority. And so the rules of publishing are in constant flux, changing with the whims of the big guys. Jon Sievert, President of the Bay Area Independent Publishers Association says "The publishing industry as a whole is something of a closed industry. They have very specific things they want to publish. If a book isn't going to sell X number of copies, they don't want to deal with it. It's much like the movie business. Someone may have a good idea, but since it's never been proven they're not going to take the chance.

"Then there are incidents like HarperCollins' (US) summer 1997 decision to cancel more than 100 books it had promised to publish. HarperCollins even demanded that writers return their advances. No apologies."

Venise Wagner, Bay Area journalist,
Media-Alliance (US)

The second, and main criticism, is the financial aspect. Bookselling appears to be far less about a book's merit and far more about the budget behind it. For a cool £25–40,000, Asda will give a title a prime display launch – but very few publishers have this kind of buying power. This is only one form of promotional budget in a sea of booksellers charging huge sums to promote books. Therefore, the only books the customers see are the ones with the big budgets behind them. This is not democratic, and it squeezes out the independents.

"A few years ago, Macmillan paid me a respectable advance for my first novel, The Marble Kiss. They then spent nothing on marketing or publicising the book. Unsurprisingly, despite admiring reviews, the book failed to sell. If this is what happens when Macmillan does pay out an advance, God knows what will happen when it doesn't, as proposed in its New Writers Scheme.
"Publishing is a business, and publishers only get behind books they invest in. Likewise, bookshops only push titles that have investment

behind them." Jay Rayner, Letters to The Guardian entitled Publish and Be Doomed

(permission to reprint fee waivered)

In defence of publishers...

The issues in the industry are manifold and deep-rooted, with margins being squeezed on many sides. The publishers themselves are concerned that despite their intense activity on a book, they sign away so much of the profit to distributors and book-sellers.

Publishers suffer from a shrinking window of display

The window of time that books are displayed in bookshops is shrinking which is not giving value for money on publisher advertising spends, and they are not recouping their investments. This will only undermine how much is spent on future book launches, unless the 'name' is big enough to guarantee return on investment. Recent 'book culls' by the major book-sellers have affected publishers badly.

Publishers suffer from lost copyright revenue

A big revenue stream for publishers traditionally has been copyright, and the ease of digital file transfer, text access and download also reduces the amount of revenue coming back into the business. This is particularly the case in Academic and Education texts where online research and download means that the legal world (preparing cases) and education world (preparing classes) are not buying the same volume of text books. This is being further exacerbated by Googleprint and Amazon's Search Inside which scan 100% of the text, whilst only releasing around 20% of it. This is allegedly often sufficient for the reader to avoid the need to buy the book - yet the author receives no percentage return.

This practice is rationalised by the fact that sales often result from the free search, and there are many supporters of this theory. Authors need to make up their own minds and decide accordingly if they want their text searchable and downloadable for free.

Publishers suffer lost revenue through heavy discounting

Heavy discounting at point of sale is passed back to the publisher in one way or another. This forces the pace in publishers needing to buy print in such volume runs as to enable massive price reductions, which means publishers need to focus on big names and mass-market chick-lit and celebrity biographies which will guarantee big sales – which exacerbates the very problem they are criticised and blamed for, that they too often go for 'big ticket' books and don't put enough effort into developing quality literature.

Publishing has a long supply chain

The publishing industry has reputedly always been a low margin business, and the emergence of new forms of printing, distribution and selling has not impacted on this positively. None of the technologies have eradicated any middle-men, they have just changed who those middle-men are. The profit margin to the author and publisher still remain the smallest part of the pie.

Where is the real money in the book trade?

The following table sets out who gets what on the price of a book (assuming a £10 price). What this reveals to us is that the real money on a per unit basis is in controlling the outlet to the customer (either high street or an online bookshop). This provides a far higher income per unit than any other part of the book publishing and selling process.

Manufacturing costs	15%	ie. £1.50
Trade Discount	55%	ie. £5.50
Distribution/Marketing	8%	ie. £0.80
Publishers Overheads	9%	ie. £0.90
Royalties	8%	ie. £0.80
Publishers Net Profit	5%	ie. £0.50

Source: The Author (Tim Hely Hutchinson)
BA Reports Library, September 1998

It is evident that authors pay dearly for being displayed – whether in the high street or via the internet. Amazon Advantage actually takes 60% which leaves the author with very little after production costs. This is the reason that so many parts of the industry have to focus on volume and scale. Production costs go down and profits go up. It makes good business sense – but independent authors suffer as a result. Short print runs have a high cost per unit, and limited routes to market can result in low sales. Independent authors must work hard indeed to reach their audience in adequate volume.

Where does it leave the author?

Authors sign away 88–92% of their royalties with a mainstream contract. This is a huge percentage when you consider that most authors agree that it is difficult to write a good book in under six months. A recent calculation showed that new authors earn a salary that, when averaged out over a year, totals nothing more than pennies per hour.

But for all this percentage handed to the publishers, the publishing houses advise that the more marketing and publicity the authors undertake, the greater the potential for return. This puts authors in a dilemma. You can't afford to give up the day job, but if you don't throw yourself wholesale into self-promotion, you won't make it as a writer.

The high percentages taken by the bookshops and distributors are exacerbated by the high discounting which is shouldered by the publisher and the author. New and midlist authors rarely have much budget spent on them, but now with the 'window of instore presence' getting shorter and shorter, returns on authoring are getting slimmer.

There are too many books out there!

Everybody in the industry is watching the changes, and commenting loudly where they have the opportunity and platform to do so – and being an industry populated by so many writers, there are many rich veins of script. Author Hillel Halkin's jokey words have more than a ring of truth to them:

"We should declare a 100 year moratorium on all new book writing so readers can catch up with what's already out there."

This would certainly suit some. Robert McCrum (Literary Editor of *The Observer*) does not believe that the increase in volume provides greater reading material, and there are many who would agree. Unedited works by new writers rarely provide literary masterpieces:

"The increase in the quantity of books over the last 10 years has not resulted in a proportional increase in the quantity of quality literature. It just means that everything is making it into the market."

Although others would disagree:

"Of the 46,000 submissions to the Richard & Judy writing competition, Macmillan were really impressed with the standard which, in terms of literacy, was high. "We are publishing six submissions rather than just one," said Maria Rejt of Macmillan. "Hopefully this will herald the democratisation of publishing." Arts Telegraph 27/7/05

The fact is there ARE too many books out there, but this is not a negative. It means that there is a much wider choice for readers and this is a good thing. The volume of the industry is actually increasing, which is a good thing. What the industry is bemoaning is that the high volume of sales are spread across a much wider range of books, and therefore it is harder to make a huge profit out of individual titles. The profit comes from selling fewer of a wider range of titles, which can only benefit self-publishers as their book sales mingle with mainstream published books – similar to what is happening in the music industry now.

Is publishing slowly becoming a meritocracy?

With the increasing range of titles for authors too choose from, and the myriad ways they can find and buy books now, bookselling is slowly becoming merit-based. When one publisher produces a "Jamie Oliver" suddenly everyone does, and shoppers can pick and choose, and few shoppers are looking at the spine to check whether it was published by a mainstream house. If the book looks professional and promising, they will buy it.

Equally there has been a sea-change in how publishers look for and find undiscovered gems that previously may have slipped through the net.

"On the whole, masterpieces tend not to fall through the net but, as Maria Rejt (Macmillan) pointed out, publishers and agents are all human and things do slip through their fingers… but there is a feeling in the air that more and more editors are not so reliant on agents for all their material… the independents produce brave and original books that mainstream publishing might not risk. Who knows? Maybe in the current climate of raised antennae, eyes and ears wider open to the great, unpublished unwashed, publishers and booksellers alike will be turning up more

unlikely gems from more unlikely authors than ever before. And if they get it right, those authors, their readers and the industry, big and the small, all stand to benefit."

The Telegraph 27/7/05 "Slush pile superstars"

Publishing is clearly experiencing its own "democratisation", but how will it happen? What shape and form will it take? Is self-publishing the answer, using all the emerging technologies and routes to market? What does it mean to the independent author? The answers to all these questions are made clear throughout this book and its partner title, "What do I have to do to sell a book!"

The independent sector must actively promote the democratisation of publishing

FACTS ABOUT THE BRITISH READING PUBLIC

The problem with publishing today is three-fold:

(i) there are too many books
(ii) there is too little time to read books
(iii) there are too many other leisure activities competing for that leisure time.

Allegedly, less than 10% of people buy books regularly (ie. over 15 books a year) whilst many only buy books for their annual holiday, and a staggering 40% of the British public never read. Indeed, 30 million people did not buy a single book in 2001. Instead, they occupy their leisure time with more 'immediate gratification' activities such as watching films and TV, playing computer games or surfing the internet.

With so many new titles last year alone and a national backlist totalling millions, not to mention access to other English-language titles worldwide available on Amazon, there is an excess of books fighting for a very small regular readership. The real struggle for readers is HOW to find what they want to read. The noise around a mass-market title with a big budget behind it is so loud that nobody can hear the individual.

Who is reading what?

Book Marketing Limited is continually researching the question of how people choose their reading material. Here are some answers, taken from BML's research entitled *"Expanding the market"*:

- On average, respondents to research read for abut 26 minutes a day; with women reading more material and reading for longer
- 38% of men were non-readers

- Book reading is highest amongst
  - the 55-64 years age range and the retired
  - those from the AB social grade (82%)
  - those still in education (85%)
  - those whose terminal education age was 19+ (79%)
- The biggest barrier to increasing reading is TIME. We're all too busy. Newspapers and magazines are increasingly the reading material of choice because they are easy, can be read in snippets and keep you up to date and informed.
- Barriers to reading as a choice of pastime include disinterest and boredom with the pace of events unfolding, unlike films where you get the action and plot quickly. This is prevalent in the under-25s, who also have difficulty finding books they want to read.
- Ease of selection – finding what you want to read – is a huge barrier to reading. Many disliked the back jackets that rave about the book without saying anything about it.
- For light-readers, paperbacks were seen as average to fair value for money, whilst hardbacks were not very good value for money; whereas medium readers had a more positive image of both.
- Trade paperbacks are rapidly replacing hardbacks for fiction; hardbacks are more expensive to produce and harder to sell.

Source: Book Marketing Ltd
www.bookmarketing.co.uk

To analyse this further... 26 minutes a day is a ridiculously short amount of time although I do not doubt this figure for a second. Publishing is competing against so many other forms of leisure activities that simply weren't available even 30 years ago, let alone a hundred years ago. Television, computers, digital games and web-surfing, music and portable systems/headphones, incessant communication via phones, texts, emails etc. We never get a chance to pause, to think, to have some quiet time, to just chill and read for a while. We live with constant stimulation and bombardment. Nowhere is private. I sit at my desk surrounded by a desk computer with two screens and a laptop, both of which have email, msn and skype; I have one landline and two mobiles and I wonder why I never get anything done.

Other leisure activities are the book industry's biggest threats

Reading takes time. It takes concentration and focus to allow the story to embrace and transport you; space to allow the characters to come to life and live amongst you. But how is this all possible in today's world; our attention is preyed upon from all quarters, and our free time is squeezed by ever-longer working hours. No wonder stress-related diseases like cancer and heart-attack are on the increase, and it should be no surprise that book reading is highest amongst the retired. Nobody else has time!

How do shoppers choose a book?

Plot synopsis	53%
Quotes on jacket	12%
Opening pages	10%
Design of cover	9%
Advertisements in the shop	2%
Pictures	2%
Don't know	13%

Source: The Way We Read:
BA Reports Library; March 2003

Once you've clambered over the above hurdles and written a book which provides fast pace and rapid character identification, then you have to make it jump off the shelf. The jacket is king. The back text is critical. It has a huge influence to the customer browsing in bookshops in the high street

Further data in the public domain reveals another dilemma… if readers have heard of you before, then you have nearly a one-third greater chance of selling a book. This makes it even harder for the first time author to get found - and even more important to get the cover to speak for itself.

People DO judge a book by its cover

What does this mean to the independent author?

It is increasingly harder to get into the high street, and "What do I have to do to sell a book!" investigates further how to get your book into the supply chain channels and how you raise awareness of your book.

The purpose of this book is to reiterate to authors the importance of publishing a book that the trade want to sell and end-readers want to buy - and exactly what this means.

SUMMARY

The abolition of the NBA combined with emerging technologies has triggered an incredible amount of change on the publishing industry, leaving it in chaos.

There is a surfeit of books and this makes it a buyers market. We are a world profuse with opinion and the ability to share it, yet people have little time to linger over reading matter. Too many other leisure activities clamour for people's attention.

There has never been a better time to self-publish – the opportunities abound

There is an increasing need to sell in high volume to return decent profits, yet few titles can achieve this mass-market scale. Most books sell in the thousands, not the hundred thousands, which squeezes publishers even further.

Fewer authors financially gain from their writing. Too many publishers are forced to focus on the bottom line yet supermarkets are seizing profits on mass-market books, undermining further the investment publishers can make on more risky or niche titles. Booksellers can dictate what they take and the terms on which they take books. They can charge handsomely for the privilege of being included in promotions, displays and visible sitings

There has never been a better time to self-publish!

There are many routes to publication today; the independent author can easily produce a high quality book if he knows what he is doing.

More and more authors are turning to self-publishing and seizing control, tired of earning nothing from their hard work and original thought.

Self-publishing is increasingly providing the opportunity for authors to prove their worth. The excess of choice means that books can be a bestseller even on a relatively low sales figure.

Individuals cannot rise above a global corporation or national conglomerates - but they can sneak underneath! Small and independent publishers can react quicker and in a more direct and focussed fashion.

The future for publishing is merit-based - just like the music industry. Consumers do not want to be force-fed mass market material, but want to choose it for themselves. Modern technology enables them to do this.

Many authors today are coming to the conclusion that it is time for them to take control and exploit the vast opportunities available to them today to write, publish and sell their books.

Self-publishing and self-selling has arrived.

Further information

The Bookseller : www.theBookseller.com
theBookseller.com is the online business information service for the book business. It provides daily updates on industry news, bestseller charts, career opportunities and market information services.

The Booksellers Association : www.booksellers.org.uk
The Bookseller's Association promotes and looks after the interests of booksellers. The site contains information on all aspects of book retailing, a searchable database of all BA members, a chatroom and offers the opportunity for BA members to purchase products.

Book Marketing Ltd : www.bookmarketing.co.uk
Established in 1990, BML is the leading company in the UK providing specialist information for and about the book industry. In particular, its knowledge and range of information on the consumer book market is unparalleled.

Booktrust : www.booktrust.org.uk

Brings books and people together. Booktrust runs book prizes and brilliant projects to encourage readers of all ages and cultures to discover and enjoy books and reading. A member of the National Book Committee, dedicated to the well-being of books and the written word. Sign-up for an e-mail newsletter.

Publishing Training Centre : www.train4publishing.co.uk
The Publishing Training Centre runs approximately 160 training courses each year as well as in-company and long distance programmes. Their website contains general information about services and details of specific courses which can be booked online.

Society of Authors : www.writers.org.uk/society
The Society of Authors advises members on the business aspects of writing. Their website outlines their main activities and benefits of membership.

The Publishers Association : www.publishers.org.uk
The Publishers Association is the leading trade organisation serving book, journal and electronic publishers in the UK. It brings publishers together to discuss the main issues facing the industry and to define the practical policies that will take the industry forward.

Scottish Publishers Association : www.scottishbooks.org
The Scottish Publishers Association (SPA) is a trade association of almost 80 Scottish publishers. Founded in 1973, they assist their members with the marketing of their books to the widest possible readership within the UK and overseas. On members' behalf, they attend many national and international book fairs and exhibitions.

Welsh Books Council : www.wbc.org.uk
The Welsh Books Council is a national body, funded by the Welsh Assembly Government, which provides a focus for the publishing industry in Wales. It provides a number of specialist services with a view to improving standards of book production and publication in both Welsh and English.

The Irish Book Publishers' Association :
www.publishingireland.com
CL... was founded in 1970 as a response to the need felt by publishers to share expertise and resources in order to benefit from opportunities and solve problems. It comprises most of the major publishing houses in Ireland with a mixture of trade, general, legal, and academic publishers as members.

The Writer's Guild of Great Britain:
www.writersguild.org.uk
The Writers' Guild of Great Britain is the union for all professional writers working in television, radio, film, theatre, books and multimedia. The Guild works to improve terms and conditions for book writers and there is an active Books Committee which organises events and seminars to help members share experiences and learn about issues of common concern.

PART II

TRADITIONAL ROUTES INTO PUBLISHING

The purpose of this chapter is to look at the traditional routes into publishing. Many authors still choose to follow the traditional routes to the market for a multitude of reasons, and this section seeks to advise how authors can maximise their opportunities here.

LITERARY AGENTS

There are around 170 literary agents as listed in the Handbooks. Rumour has it that without a literary agent you won't find a publisher… without being previously published, you won't find a literary agent… and most literary agents and publishing houses claim not to read unsolicited manuscripts. The vicious circle of rejection.

In reality, publishers do receive unsolicited manuscripts, although sometimes suspend this service temporarily due to workload; and literary agents imply they are not receiving, but closer inspection reveals they just don't receive manuscripts that don't adhere to their submission guidelines.

Some literary agents are very small one-man bands; others are large organisations of 50-100 people. Some specialise in certain genres or fields, and others are general representatives. Irrespective of their specialisations or generalisations, literary agents will only take on authors whose work they believe in. If they believe your work has intrinsic literary qualities and a commercial potential, they will represent you. If they don't believe in your work, they won't.

Good agents will have good inside knowledge of the categories in which they specialise.

When literary agents sign up a new author, they are staking their professional reputation on you, your ability to deliver and your ability to help sell and market yourself as an author. They do not charge money up front (although some might charge reading fees), but represent you on an agreed percentage which is paid to them after they have invested a LOT of time on you and your book/s and only when they have secured a publishing contract. It is increasingly hard for agents to earn a reliable income nowadays as the average publisher's advance decreases, and fewer, but much larger advances are offered. Therefore, the percentage is usually 15% in the UK and 20% in the US.

What do agents actually do?

Agents represent authors' careers whereas publishers publish and sell the book. They critically assess your work and define the elements that make the author and his/her writing marketable. They then nurture these elements, guiding and directing the author and often-times editing the book or book idea. NB Not all agents edit – some leave this process to the publisher. Agents also advise on current publishing trends.

Once they are ready, having carefully laid the ground, literary agents will professionally submit the work to editors who have been handpicked from their knowledge of publisher's lists and editors' tastes. They then represent and negotiate the sale of that work to the best publisher.

Agents spend time with their authors, whereas publishers rarely see them.

"Best" does not necessarily mean the highest bid! A publisher might win the work for a variety of factors. Advances are important, but so are marketing plans. A publisher making a bid for this and the author's next work will get to the top of the pecking order when literary agents are deciding to whom to award the work. Obviously, this is only the case on a very hot property, which is rare, but in most cases the work will be submitted on an editor-by-editor basis until one bites. Their reputation contributes enormously to the submission. Invariably agents also handle the American, foreign and serial rights as well as ancillary rights, such as merchandising and film and television.

Agents also act as an ear to authors, and a mouthpiece for them. Being a writer can be an extremely solitary existence and the relationship between author and agent is intimate and honest. An agent can advise on early ideas, help with writer's block, be a sounding board and a punch bag; they advise on tours, travel and signings, royalty statements, special sales, promotions, etc. Also, the agent can do the jobs the author doesn't want to, thereby leaving the author and editor free to talk only about the book eg. if the author absolutely hates a cover and is too scared to complain to the publisher about it, often the agent gets sent it to do the dirty work – as it were!

Needless to say, agents spend a lot of time with their authors whereas many published authors say that they rarely see their publisher. It is a very time-consuming business for an agent to nurture, train, direct and sell an author, which makes the choice of author even more critical.

Getting an agent

If the agent likes the sample chapters, they'll call for the whole manuscript. If they like the manuscript, they might call the author in for a chat because it's important that author and agent like each other.

The instinct is for authors to start searching for an agent the moment they qualify from a Master's in creative writing, or have completed the first novel they are proud of. But authors should not be tempted to start submitting to agents widely just because they've finished a novel. Seek endorsement or a critique from an independent editor first (see Writing and Editorial Services on page 173).

What should an *author* be looking for in an *agent*?

Authors should be looking for an agent that they trust and they like, but also an agent who has the best contacts in the author's genre. Agents have portfolios just like publishers have portfolios. I'm sure many authors reading this book will have received the response 'not quite right for our list' from agents in the past. There is little point in submitting a crime novel to an agent specialising in children's books.

Different literary agents *may* focus on different elements of publishing ie. the creative aspect of the writing versus the editorial; some may pay close attention to career planning whilst others throw energy into the marketing and promoting of book and author. But, ultimately, most agents offer a similar service - they exist to get publishing contracts. How much they help, edit, hand-hold is really up to the specific personality of the agent and the sort of relationship they end up developing with their authors. *"I have quite different relationships with all my clients because they're all different people!"* advises Penny Holroyde of The Caroline Sheldon Literary Agency.

Penny Holroyde's advice

"In a nutshell, I would advise authors to pay attention to the submission guidelines as printed by the agent in the yearbooks... cover letters and synopses should be well crafted; work should be neatly presented, typed on single-sided paper and double-spaced; sufficient postage should be enclosed in case of return; do not call the agent chasing for a response and don't send the manuscript out to hundreds of agents at once, but handpick one two.

"These are all relatively standard submission guideline requests, but you'd be amazed how many authors choose to ignore these."

Penny Holroyde,
Caroline Sheldon Literary Agency

Why would you choose to approach an agent?

Literary agents remain the Holy Grail of successful publishing, and many successfully self-published authors acknowledge this once they are signed up with an agent. They are expert in the industry, they provide valuable endorsement of your work and abilities as an author and, most of all, they manage your career in areas where you have least knowledge. For the unpublished writer, the best route today to securing an agent is to establish a value for your work. Get an independent critique; submit only the best material and follow the guidelines. If this doesn't work for you but you still crave a career as a writer, then consider throwing all that energy into self-publishing. Get out there and prove your worth. If it's successful, the agents will find you.

LARGE / CONGLOMERATE PUBLISHING HOUSES

There are hundreds of publishers out there, ranging from the sole trader to the global conglomerate. There are twelve major publishing conglomerates today, who have descended and merged together from the 30 major publishing houses of the first half of the twentieth century. The last fifty years have seen the birth of successful, new publishing independents, some of whom have then been bought out and become imprints of the conglomerates.

These conglomerates excel at scale ie. selling high volume bestsellers because of their sheer buying power.

It is popular and common knowledge that publishers receive hundreds of manuscripts per week, most of which receive an 'acid test' assessment ie. read the first paragraph, read a chunk of dialogue in the middle, read the synopsis... whatever. Each reader has their own method for assessing a manuscript for the Rejection or For Consideration pile. What all publishing houses are united in saying is:

"It has to be very good to make the grade, and much of what comes in is not very good."

The conglomerates reportedly publish hundreds of new titles per year whilst taking on only a handful of new authors; the rest are established authors.

What publishers do

Publishers fulfil the many tasks required to take a manuscript from original form to final copy, making it available in shops and online for sale. This comprises many skilled roles such as editing, design, typesetting, printing etc, as well as hundreds of little, but important tasks. Further on in the book is a chart which endeavours to summarise the key elements of the process (see pages 128/129). This has been kept as succinct and relevant as possible as it pertains to the self-publishing author, and there are other books on the market that explore the process of mainstream publishing in far more depth.

Conglomerates have buying power and global reach, often owning businesses in other countries of the world. Whilst you may get overlooked as an unknown or midlist author, as a bestselling author you will benefit from their size.

Another area of work that the publishers and agents implement – and one that authors often forget about or totally overlook – is the selling of rights. The income generated from the sale of various different rights is a large revenue stream to a publisher, and is thus very important to the business. Obviously, as a self-publishing author you are more restricted on how much revenue you may generate from this source.

What they don't do

What publishers won't do is, in short, to take a poorly written manuscript or an average idea and do the work for the author. The submitted work has to be good and have many redeeming features.

How the conglomerates work

Conglomerates ultimately have to look to the bottom line as they are corporations like any others. They publish across a range of genres, often categorised under imprints. They monitor publishing trends and seek titles that capture the biggest audiences. Whilst in many cases this means mass-market famous people biographies, chicklit and crime thriller – as well as the popular trends of cookery and home make-

Publishers are less likely to take on your book if they cannot see the market potential

over titles – this doesn't necessarily rule out more exploratory new literary titles. However, if your book is difficult to categorise, they are less likely to run with it.

Conglomerates tend to have a high turnover of titles, which can also translate as a high turnover of authors. There are 140,000 new titles released each year yet the average-sized bookshop stocks only 30,000 titles at any given time.

Publishers see first time authors as the greatest risk.

In order to remain competitive and ahead of the game, conglomerates ensure they maintain a set ratio of established and reliable authors who sell well, and new authors who can provide interest and excitement. This means that there is plenty of opportunity for new authors; the industry is not actually a closed shop, although many would accuse it of being so. What this does mean is that books have an increasingly small window of opportunity to find their audience before they are remaindered.

Large publishers have three selling cycles per year which is largely driven by the booksellers who seek to keep a 'lively and interesting environment'. Booksellers are increasingly working like fashion outlets, replacing stock in tune with the seasons and key dates in the annual calendar. New books are therefore invariably displayed for a 4 month period before they are either returned to the publisher, or put onto the shelves should they provide a low, but steady turnover. Only 30% of new books will sell well with another 30% selling badly. The remaining books may only break even.

One shot one season… Many news books only receive a 4 month display

This means that pre-marketing and launch activity is such a critical time for a new book. Authors would be well advised to clear the diary of any form of interruption and other responsibilities. Get out there and sell for all you are worth whilst there is support and momentum from the industry. It is your one chance.

Initial print runs will vary between 1,000-10,000 (averaging somewhere in between) and a book will be supported by the publisher for its first year. If it does well, the book will get reprinted and more promotional money will be spent on it.

Allegedly, publishers work on the 80/20 rule whereby 20% of the business gets 80% of the attention and support. In practice, many publishers would disagree and say it is not as straightforward as this. One thing is obvious, however; the more money that is spent on promotion, the more readers will be aware of the book - and very few books receive any real marketing. Many books don't make it past their first year of publication and end up being remaindered, sold off to the author at cost or pulped.

Publishing houses work on the premise "you're only as good as your last book". Even if your first few books have sold well, they are quick not to renew the contract if the last book didn't sell so well. Louise Voss experienced this. After a six-figure advance fanfare, her first two books sold extremely well.

"I had a great agent and was signed onto Transworld with a large advance. They gave me all the promotion and marketing that they promised - poster campaigns on the underground, reviews in the media, sold extracts, wrote features etc - and the first book did very well. The second book received far less advertising and no publicity, which had a direct impact on the contract for the next two books, which was much lower. In retrospect (and seeing how the industry is developing at the moment) I understand that even being offered a second contract demonstrated their belief in me. Yet neither of the next two books had any serious promotional budget behind them, and as a result the books just didn't sell as well. At most, these two books made it onto the 3 for 2 promotion tables for a couple of weeks.

"Books can't sell without the awareness being driven from somewhere. Additionally, it has to be meaningful promotion. Upon reflection, my first book should have done better, given the amount of money spent on it. But was it spent correctly?

"When a publisher signs you on with a big advance, you know you are going to get some decent publicity, as they need to ensure a return on investment. Looking back, I think I made one big mistake which was not to allow them to parade the large advance, which prohibited any real pre-marketing - not that I heard anyone advising me any differently."

Ergo, if you are only being given an advance of a few thousand, then you know you won't necessarily get the investment at the marketing end of the process.

Summary

There are plenty of opportunities for authors if they are prepared to play their role within the process:

- Write something new; even if the topic has been previously covered, make sure you present new information, a different or perspective.
- Know what category you would expect to see this book fitting into - look on Amazon, go into your local bookshop.
- Spend time researching what publishers are looking for.
- State the message of your book clearly, so the media have a chance to hear it clearly.

It's hard work, driven largely by passion rather than real return, except for a handful of authors. Authors would be well advised to truly understand the publishing process in order to maximise their opportunities. This book seeks to give in depth information and guidance if you choose

There is plenty of opportunity for new authors in today's market.

to self-publish. If you wish to read more about how a large publishers, there is a list of books below that will provide more comprehensive information.

Further information:

An Author's Guide to Publishing by Michael Legat
Since the previous revision many changes have taken place in the publishing world, not least the abandonment of the Net Book Agreement and the developments in electronic publishing. Good advice as well as a useful account of the publishing process and its structure is presented in this 3rd edition which has been extensively rewritten and reset.
ISBN: 0709062273

The Truth about Publishing by Stanley Unwin
Reprint of the much revised 7th edition (1960) of Sir Stanley's classic treatise.
ISBN: 1558214232

INDEPENDENT PUBLISHERS

Firstly, a few facts:

- There are 385 listed members of the Independent Publishers Guild; these are not self-publishers, but small, independently-owned publishers, who between them share an annual turnover of £350m.
- 30% of independent publishers are very small ie. turning over less than £100k per annum. Given the high cost base of book production, this is VERY low. Only 5% earn over £5m per annum.
- Most independent publishers are very small, with 80% of them employing less than 10 people.

It is reported that independent publishing is where the new, innovative talent is nurtured. It is said that they bring variety to a market that would, if left just to the conglomerates, become dominated by a handful of leading authors, desired largely by the mass-market. The conglomerates are far more driven by the need to achieve volume sales, therefore they go with already successful formulas – the author name, the genre.

> **"The future of publishing is in the hands of the independent publisher."**
> *Carole Blake, Blake Friedmann*

Carole Blake, of literary agency Blake Friedmann, criticised the short-termism of conglomerates, and believes that the future of publishing is in the hands of the independent. *"Whilst advances may be smaller, the independents provide far greater care and innovation."*

Andrew Franklin, of the successful independent publishing house Profile, is not so sure. *"If you look at some of the fantastic material, as well as the breadth of material, at a large conglomerate, you will realise this simply isn't the case. The large publishing houses take as many 'risks' as the small independents."*

Yet in the last year, a couple of independent publishers have done very nicely thank you from authors such as Yann Martel (Canongate), Lynne Truss (Profile) and Alexander McCall Smith (Polygon Edinburgh). Publishers such as these took on slightly riskier titles and won… after all, who would have thought the British Reading Public wanted to read about Botswana's first lady detective? Whilst some of these authors were previously successfully published, the title they achieved most recognition for is the one rejected by the conglomerates. For Yann Martel, it was his own belief in the title partnered with the support of the independent publisher that drove it through onto the market. Lynne Truss had been published previously with Faber & Faber, but achieved most success with *Eats, Shoots & Leaves* published by Profile.

Where the independents suffer most is in the distribution unless they use the distribution services of a conglomerate. Good distribution is costly because it is so disparate nowadays, and it is now common practice for publishing houses to pay for inclusion in bookshop promotions, catalogues and window displays. Not only do small publishers pay a higher cost per unit at print (because they are publishing smaller runs), but the independent can pay as much as four times more on distribution than a large publisher and the price wars between supermarkets and bookstores hit the independent publisher badly. All that work can result in only pennies being returned per book sold, and new authors would be wise to remember that there is virtually no margin on books except in volume sales.

Andrew Franklin doesn't dispel this thought. *"Most publishers don't make money,"* he shrugs. *"When they do, it is on a handful of titles."*

Profile publish non-fiction because they believe this is where the meaningful stories come from. *"Why do people write?"* Andrew asks rhetorically. *"Generally because they have survived some dreadful experience or witnessed a shocking injustice. When their story is told well, it acts as a learning to others, even if just to be grateful for their own lot! We gain more from fact than we do from fiction, and this is where I believe the real value of story-telling comes from. However, it is not fair to say that the independents have a monopoly on this, and it is not fair to say that conglomerates only churn out mass-market and only the independents nurture new talent. The only difference between the two is that the smaller, independent publisher probably has more fun. It's a tighter team with easier communication channels and greater flexibility."*

Certainly when you read through Profile's catalogues, you get the feeling that every single book has been written from the heart and produced with a matching passion. The catalogue has been produced as lovingly as each book undoubtedly has been, and clearly produced with one strong, authoritative voice - Andrew Franklin's. Despite all his protests that there is no real difference between conglomerate and independent, his catalogue contradicts this. Someone has spent time on it, and time is short in corporations. This has been signed off by one voice, which doesn't generally happen in corporations.

Andrew concludes his view of the industry by saying that the problem with the book industry at the moment is two-fold. Firstly, there are simply too many books being produced - most of which are rubbish - and secondly, the value of books is shockingly low. This begs the question as to whether independents should call for a reinstatement of a "net book agreement", or at the very least moratorium periods on discounting?

Choosing a publisher – conglomerate versus independent

The overriding fact is that authors are not in a position to discriminate except on political grounds; and very few do. An author just wants a publisher, irrespective of size. However, for authors who desire to discriminate on a point of principle or authors who are in the enviable position to pick and choose, you might conclude the following.

Authors reportedly receive a greater attention to detail, care and nurturing from an independent publisher. The smaller publisher is likely to take on riskier, more niche titles and can make independent choices to nurture author's careers in the longer term as they are not answerable to a team of accountants or shareholders.

Larger publishers excel at scale and, if you wish to aim for a couple of big launches to the mass-market and see what bites, you may prefer to start pitching to the big publishers first.

Authors may therefore conclude that who they approach at the outset will mirror their objectives.

Further information

Independent Publishers Guild: www.ipg.uk.com
The Independent Publishers Guild (IPG) is the membership organisation for independent publishing companies. The primary purposes of the IPG are to promote knowledge about publishing and to provide members with a forum for the exchange of ideas and information

Phone: 01763 247014
Email: info@ipg.uk.com

"But... how does anyone find my manuscript?"

Just as there is a surfeit of books on the market, there is an even bigger surfeit of unpublished books behind the scenes.

The big publishing houses receive circa one thousand manuscripts per week. To process all of these would cost the company a fortune, and, given that many do not fit the publisher's line or are badly written, it simply is not cost effective to do so. Sometimes manuscripts are returned unread, although most publishers advise that an initial assessment or check *is* undertaken before issuing a pre-printed rejection letter.

Many publishers do not accept unsolicited manuscripts and have deferred this responsibility onto the literary agents. However, the literary agents are invariably very small businesses without the staff to trawl through manuscripts, particularly as many authors just randomly send material out to all and sundry, or have not had the work professionally assessed prior to submitting it. Ergo, the slush mountain grows.

The slush pile problem:

1. the slush pile is too big
2. the quality is too often too low
3. the selling potential for most is too small
4. the expense to assess them all is too high
5. the chance of a publisher finding a gem is too slim.

What's the answer?

Publishers and agents alike bemoan the fact that too much material is written that is either low-grade, inappropriate for today and/or has no real audience out there. And this is where authors must take their responsibility.

The author must ensure that his story is well-plotted and the text is well edited; authors would be wise to have their work independently assessed prior to submitting it as only the very best makes it through.

Authors must do their homework and find out what publishers are likely to be interested. *"But this information is impossible to find out!"* goes the cry. It is difficult, yes, but impossible, no; and this is discussed further on page 66 *"But how do I find the right people to send my manuscript to?"*

The author must also demonstrate clearly and precisely who he is aiming his book at, why he has written it and what the benefit is. Make your pitch and sell it to a publisher - give it the best shot.

Will this guarantee me being found?

Not necessarily, but if authors make an initial investment into their manuscript, everyone potentially benefits. There are smaller slush piles comprising better quality material; literary agents have a better chance of finding this material and publishers can focus on producing the highest quality of product. Literary agents and publishers may even have time to watch the self-publishing market to spot new talent.

Whilst authors feel that the publishing industry is completely out of their control, the fact is that they initiate the whole process. If authors take the responsibility to produce a well-written, well edited book, they are more likely to succeed - and you are better poised to turn to self-publishing if you haven't taken the rejection slips to heart.

ADVICE & GUIDANCE

The advice from the industry came thick and fast during my research, and the general consensus of opinion is that authors generally do not do enough to help themselves. Here are a host of words of advice from the industry.

"Practice in private"
Robert McCrum, Literary Editor, The Observer

Don't feel the need to rush out and get an agent or publisher immediately, but research your market and target it accurately. Only when your manuscript is endorsed by a professional editor with a track record and credible reputation, are you truly ready to start approaching the market. And whilst self-publishing is a route open to everyone at the outset, the majority of authors prefer to approach the literary agents and publishing houses first.

The reason for this is partly because the author doesn't have to fund publication when following this route, but often equally important is the "endorsement" factor. The potential worth of anything artistic is often difficult to evaluate, and authors need an outside expert to tell them if their work is any good. If a publisher takes you on, they are basically endorsing your abilities as a writer; they are staking their reputation on your potential and are providing you with the power of the brand name. This is all very motivating and important stuff. So be sure your 'baby' is ready for scrutiny before you start the hard slog to find a buyer.

All you need is one person who believes in your work – the trick is to find them.

The best reference points for information are of course *The Writer's Handbook* and *The Writers' & Artists' Yearbook* and these offer slightly differing information and advice. It is worth investing in both, and ensuring you buy the most recent edition as the publishing world is a fast-moving one - and by that I mean the people within it move jobs very quickly!

"Create well-written material"

Telling a compelling story is a rare and inherent talent - just like the ability to sing pitch perfect with no training and play like Beethoven when you are deaf. Shakespeare never had lessons, nor did Tolkien. However, this is a RARE skill. For the rest of us, we need to practise our art by reading widely and copiously, by writing and gaining independent assessment.

The main point here is to know why you are writing the book and why anyone should read it. Understand this, and you are halfway on the road to success.

"Know what your book is about"

Most authors cannot sum up in a snappy little sentence what their book is actually about, which is the difference between being given an opportunity or not. Whilst you ramble on about the plot, the publisher or agent on the other end of your ramble is getting impatient. So Rule Number One… if you do get the opportunity to speak to a publisher or agent about your book, make sure you have the most incredibly inspiring, succinct and accurate description of the plot of your book. One sentence in less than a minute could make the difference to an invitation to submit the material, or a refusal to see it.

Write a good synopsis that sells its benefits and merits.

"Know your target market"

WRITING A GOOD SYNOPSIS: BEST PRACTICE

By Hilary Johnson

While some agents/editors have specific individual requirements for a synopsis to be submitted with a partial, most would expect this:

- Keep as far as possible to two A4 sheets, single-spaced, one sided
- Number the pages and inc. a header identifier
- 2-3 pages (but 3 only if it is a very long novel)
- Use the present tense
- Begin with a couple of sentences stating what kind of novel it is and what it is about, also when and where it is set and who it features

The remainder of the synopsis will be an encapsulation of the complete story within the proverbial nutshell. (It should not be confused with a jacket blurb. Do not talk up the novel or litter the outline with teasers or end on a cliff-hanger. The purpose of this is to enable a person permanently inundated with paper to grasp the essence of the whole story within a few minutes.) Concentrate on the key character(s) and the main plot points of the story, omitting unimportant detail, minor characters, etc. Prune unnecessary words ruthlessly. It's worth remembering that active verbs lend life to the writing and another tip is never to refer to 'the novel' but always give its title. Lastly, think of the dictum that a good novel should be a good story.

The creation of any product requires in depth research before you start the arduous task of producing it. Before you start a line of greetings cards, you would research the greetings cards market to check where the gaps are, or whether someone is already selling your concept. Books are no different. The market doesn't need another wizarding fantasy tale right now, but it does need some fact-based, interesting stories for 9–13 year olds (allegedly). Authors need to know what competitive edge their book has; ensure this is the focus of both the text and any pitches they make to a publisher/agent.

"Be in tune with the modern Zeitgeist"

Trends change. Nobody could have predicted the popularity of Lynne Truss' book on punctuation and grammar or a book on snapshots of England's history (*The Pocket Book of Patriotism*). Publishing is an industry where success is more magic than logic. The success or failure of a book is so closely related to the timing of its launch, and anything can happen. If you launch a book that is in tune with the modern Zeitgeist (the intellectual and cultural climate of an era), you are already well-poised to be noticed. This is discussed further in *"But how can anyone predict a trend or see what's the next hot topic?" on page 73*.

The publishing industry is more magic than logic.

"Send your manuscript to the right people"

If you thought that writing 60–100,000 words was hard work, then stop at this point and just carry on with the day job. The next arduous and time-consuming task is to find the one right person, who believes in the potential of your book enough to buy the rights to publishing it. Most authors believe this is done by throwing enough mud at the wall and seeing what sticks ie. send a copy of your manuscript to every publisher and agent in the Handbook / Yearbook. In reality, all this does is create a 'book mountain', making it an impossible task for anyone to find the real gems, and perpetuating the problems of the industry. The issue of knowing who to send your manuscript to is fully covered in *"But how do I find the right people to send my manuscript to?"* on page 66.

"Follow submission guidelines"

As Penny Holroyde said, most people don't follow submission guidelines, and this risky strategy can wipe out their chances before they have even started.

Some agents/publishers like to be emailed with an advance enquiry as to the suitability of submission of your material. Others prefer for you just to post it. Very, very few publishers or agents like you to phone in the first instance – if any. If you ignore their submission preferences, you will get a very short shrift. Do your homework. (See Submission Guidelines on the next page.)

> **Most authors cannot succinctly describe their own work.**

The chances are that you have tried calling an agent only to be sent away with a flea in your ear, being told to get one of the Handbooks and follow the guidelines. Don't get offended. The publishing industry operates on pretty low profit margins as books have a comparatively high cost per unit to produce and there are many middle men involved in the selling process. It was recently reported by Book Marketing Ltd that salaries in publishing industry are amongst the lowest when averaged out across the levels. Thus, many publishers and agents are struggling to do the job of two or three people (sometimes using a very outmoded paper-based system).

SUBMISSION GUIDELINES: BEST PRACTICE

By Hilary Johnson

It is essential that the typescript of a novel to be sent to agent or publisher has a professional appearance. Editors are instantly alerted by the way a typescript looks, even by the way it is packaged, to the probable quality of the material itself. Also, for people who have mountains of material to read, it is vital that the author make their task as trouble-free as possible. The following guidelines show how to do this – and contain some points which will be of use to authors working in other writing areas.

- The Title Page should give the title and the author's name – or pseudonym if one is used – centre page, the approximate number of words (rounded off) and with the author's real name, address and phone/email details bottom right corner.
- Include a covering letter, which is concise, to the point, gives any pertinent information about the author, well-written and absolutely error-free. First impressions are vital.
- The typescript must be typed in DOUBLE SPACING on one side of the paper.
- All new paragraphs/new lines of dialogue should be indented by five spaces, except the first paragraph of a new chapter or section, which should be blocked to the left-hand margin.
- Extra line spaces should not be left between paragraphs or dialogue, other than to indicate a change of location, time lapse, viewpoint shift or similar. For normal purposes, indent in the usual way.
- Do not justify the right-hand side of the text.
- Use clear print, with a good-sized plain font ie. 12 point
- Allow a good margin (about 3-4cm) all round.
- Number pages consecutively. An identifier on each page is sensible. Editors' offices can be chaotic places and, should pages become separated, this enables then to find their rightful place.
- Begin each chapter on a new page.
- Revise carefully for errors. (Grammar, spelling and punctuation DO matter!)

- DO NOT staple or pin pages together or separate chapters into plastic folders.
- DO NOT use ring binders or other fastenings. Secure the pages with an elastic band only and place in a wallet folder labelled with your name and the title. Use two folders if the ts is bulky.
- DO NOT include jacket designs, jacket blurbs, sales/promotions proposals, etc.
- Post in a NEW padded envelope. Usually the seal provided is sufficient, but a strip of ordinary sellotape will provide extra security. Remember that someone has to undo this and hundreds of other packages. They don't appreciate doing battle with staples, heavy duty fastenings or dealing with packaging damaged through over-use or inadequacy.
- Include either stamps or a cheque to cover return postage.
- Recorded/Special delivery makes work for the recipient. Keep a Proof of Posting slip for yourself and enclose a self-addressed stamped postcard for the publisher/agent to acknowledge receipt of the ts. (It need hardly be said that it is essential to keep a copy of the ts for yourself.)
- Give the agent/editor plenty of time to read your ts. Nothing ensures the rapid return of material more effectively than a pushy author!

Summary

In short, follow the guidelines. Make sure you send your submission to a 'name', typed on single-sided A4 with a covering letter:

- what it is about
- why you wrote it
- who is your intended audience
- other relevant information such as market data and marketing opportunities
- why you're qualified to write it; include your professional credentials
- your author biography – what is of public interest about you or makes you interesting/unique

"Go exclusive in the first instance"

Some publishers and agents do not want to receive material that has been posted en masse to all the publishing and literary companies, but will request exclusive submissions. If the publisher or agent is particularly desirable to you, then it would be worth your while to submit to them on an exclusive basis. However, if you have a manuscript that has been heavily praised by an independent editor and people are taking an age to respond, you may seek to spread your wings a bit wider and send out more copies. At some point, statistics will play a part.

"Be personable and PR-able"

If you get an interview, treat it like you would any pitch to sell a product – or a job interview. Know your offer. Make sure you can talk about your book engagingly and interestingly. After all, they are not only seeking to represent your book, but also to work with you.

"Deal with rejection"

Sometimes the speed with which your submission is returned to you will make your head spin, and you realise that the post office is actually remarkably efficient. But what does this rapid response mean… that it was inadvertently posted back to you with a standard "Thanks, but no thanks" slip of paper? Maybe the Assessor never saw it or hasn't had time to review it yet… therefore, should you resubmit it?

At other times, you wait so long for a response that you don't recognise your own handwriting when your SAE is finally returned to you. Does this mean that they were tempted by the book and held onto it just in case? That it has been in and out of many meetings, but finally they thought they had better make a decision one way or another in case you were waiting to send it on to the next publishing house?

Who knows, and if you phone up to ask you will get a short shrift… and you're back at the beginning again. It would be helpful if they just wrote to you honestly and said "We don't like your writing style", "the plot is weak", "the storyline is too hackneyed", or even "We don't have time to look at this and we may live to regret this in the future".

The fact is, not every publisher will either look at your submission nor want to publish on that particular subject. Don't take it personally, as many publishers have rejected valuable material. Rejection is merely the point at which you begin to look at your other alternatives.

Other good books to read

From Pitch to Publication by Carole Blake ISBN: 03337140350
Carole Blake is one of Britain's foremost literary agents and has written a marvellously detailed and accessible book, not about how to write, but, once that manuscript is typed up, how to go about getting it published.

501 Writers' questions answered by Nancy Smith
For those who want to write, on any basis, this reference book has the answer to more than 500 of the most common questions asked. Using a question and answer format, it includes advice on using a word processor, researching, presentation, copyright, and finding agents and publishers.
ISBN: 0749914971

Becoming a writer by Dorothea Brande
Describes a writer's temperament and how to develop a writer's habits, originality and insight, imitate exemplary works, read critically, and overcome writing difficulties.
ISBN: 0874771641

How to Write and Sell a Book Proposal by Stella Whitelaw
ISBN 1902713052
Whether you are a beginner or established writer, this step-by-step guide can help you structure a synopsis, plot an outline and polish your final words...from the moment of conception; through revision, synopsis creation, plotting and polishing until every word is like a diamond, honed to perfection. This invaluable guide not only shows the writer how to enjoy writing but also how to be a professional and successful writer.

"But... how do I find the right people to send my manuscript to?"

Publishing is a private club. Information is scattered and largely only available through people involved in the industry. Catalogues are a thing of the past, brochures and literature never really existed; publishers don't announce what they are looking for or what their vision is for the future and any inside knowledge about current trends remain a secret.

In order to retain competitive edge, companies must keep their knowledge secret and this is compounded by the fact that publishing is more art than science, therefore everyone needs to keep their options open. Publishers cannot afford to focus on one area and shut the door on another.

This means that new authors have to work hard indeed to find information, picking up tit-bits here and there. You need to do your research thoroughly in order to discover who deals with your subject matter – and this is hard work. Most of the conglomerates produce such a wide range of titles that their list appears disparate to the outsider. Many conglomerates have imprints which specialise in certain categories but again this information is hard for the outsider to understand. Very few publishers / imprints still produce catalogues which is a shame. These catalogues were important messages, conveying a strong overall flavour of the range of titles and well-written catalogues helped both buyers and authors.

Visiting publisher websites often turns up little more than a shopfront or promotional banners for their best-sellers or new titles. Conglomerate websites tend to present a very corporate brand image which reveals nothing of the character of the titles they produce; little effort is made to build up the brand of the individual imprints.

The entries into the Handbook / Yearbook are often little more than lists of categories; on occasion they list authors they represent.

The new author is up against it before he even starts, and in his confusion he ends up using the scattergun approach, posting his manuscript into the void with the vague hope that someone somewhere will see it and run with it.

So what you need to do is…

TIPS FOR SUCCESS

"Maximise your routes into the industry"

There are no hard and fast rules other than a few specific basics, like manuscripts should be double spaced and not bound. There are no specific 'processes' written up and everyone you encounter in the publishing world will do 'it' differently. New entrants to the publishing world just feel their way forward, bumping along and being pointed in different directions. The lack of rules provides its own charm, whilst the lack of standardisation provides a veil of secrecy.

One good way to keep yourself informed about how authors should inhabit the publishing world and maximise their chances within it, is to subscribe to the writing magazines, websites and membership centres.

"Collect memberships - join the club"

The publishing industry is old school, and in this very competitive field you need to know the ropes and the people. It is WHAT you know and WHO you know that counts. Not everyone is born knowing the contacts, but the wise will quickly make them – and yes, anyone can create contacts. It is yet another hard slog, but if you really have the burning desire to be successful and are certain you have written something worth reading, then you will immerse yourself in the business of publishing.

> **"If it looks like a duck, acts and quacks like a duck, then it IS a duck."**

"Go to the festivals and make contacts"

The Writer's Handbook has a listing of all festivals on the UK mainland, and most of these have websites announcing who is going to be where and when. The committed author will keep an eye on these and attend some of them with a view to talking to other authors (particularly in the same category of writing). Other authors, even in the same category, are incredibly supportive of new authors trying to break into publishing. They willingly share advice, offer endorsements if they like your work, share contacts, make recommendations etc. Sometimes there are representatives from publishing companies at these festivals with whom you could have a chat.

"Visit the Fairs and glean information"

Equally, authors should attend the London Book Fair. This is a trade fair. It is chaotic and frantic, and the enthusiastic new author must remember that the staff on the stands are not scouting for new authors, but are trying to sell existing titles into the trade.

What you will discover is exactly what types of books a publishing company is actively promoting and selling, and understand the character of its brand - a wall of titles in one place tells a big story. You can always ask the staff on the stand what titles are selling in volume, why, and what they might be looking for more of in the future.

Given the fact that it is so difficult to discover who does what, this can be an invaluable avenue for creating your spreadsheet of who to approach.

"Attend courses and learn more"

Who knows what sort of inspiration you will glean from going on a writing courses, or what sort of contacts you will make.

- Every summer The British Council publish an annual directory of creative-writing courses. Further information can be found on *www.britishcouncil.org/seminars*
- The Arvon Foundation in Devon run residential writing courses for new writers, songwriters, poets, novelists, script and screenwriters, playwrights, journalists and more – *www.arvonfoundation.org*.
- You've seen the ads for years... Writers Guild of GB obviously runs writing courses where you may make useful contacts as well as improve your craft – *www.writersguild.org.uk*
- Ty Newydd is the National Writers' Centre for Wales. Residential courses are held on all aspects of creative writing in both English and Welsh – visit their website: *www.tynewydd.org*

"Join a Writers' Circle and ask questions"

Visit *www.writers-circles.com* for a comprehensive list of writer's circles and workshops. The Directory started life as the Directory of Writers' Circles and then expanded to include courses. Circles often change their contact details, so every endeavour is made to give the correct information and there are now two new editions annually. As soon as a new edition is published the older ones go out of print, so you will always receive the latest edition when you order.

Previous Directories:
Directory of Writers' Circles, Courses and Workshops 2005 (Revised Edition);
ISBN 1-904065-06-6 / ISSN 1747-7247

"Enter competitions & awards"

The truly committed author immerses himself in both the publishing industry and his genre, endlessly entering the vast range of writing competitions, attending reading groups and writers' circles, visiting trade fairs and book festivals. The more you immerse yourself, the more opportunities you create for yourself.

With the recent Richard & Judy "British Book Awards" the organisers received 46,000 entries. It was intended that there would be only one winner although six contracts were ultimately issued due to the very high standard of submissions and their commercial potential.

There are new competitions being launched on a regular basis, and this is becoming yet another very viable route to market.

"Stay ahead – know what's coming up next"

To stay truly ahead of what's happening in publishing, authors should subscribe to various magazines and sign up to certain societies and online memberships. For example, *The Bookseller* is a weekly magazine about the book trade.

Publishing News is a weekly magazine, obviously about the publishing industry. There are also various monthly writing magazines – *Writer's Forum, Writers' News, Writers' Magazine, Ms Lexia* etc. They detail all of the upcoming competitions and events, as well as providing endless, helpful snippets of information about publishing work. Memberships include Society of Authors (although you need to be a published author) to join.

Can you get funding for your project?

Arts Council England is the national development agency for the arts. Between 2003 and 2006 it will invest £2 billion of public funds in the arts in England, including funding from the National Lottery. It believes that the arts have the power to transform lives and communities, and to create opportunities for people throughout the country. Go to: *www.artscouncilofengland.co.uk*

Even more information can be obtained from:

The Book Trust which publishes a Guide to Literary Prizes, listing the latest administrators and publicists. *www.booktrust.org.uk*

Another fantastic website to visit to find out loads of writing competitions is *www.firstwriter.com/competitions/*. Just fill in the fields and search ñ then get writing!

The Society of Authors manages a number of annual competitions, details of which can be found on their website ñ *www.societyofauthors.org*

If you are a crime writer, then you should become a member of the Crime Writerís Association (CWA) in order to enter in some of their competitions and awards ñ *www.thecwa.co.uk*

Bear in mind that the *Writer's Handbook* and *Writers' and Artists' Yearbook* also list competitions and awards.

"But... how can anyone predict a trend or see what's the next hot topic?"

Can anyone *predict* a trend, or is this just the rapid response of savvy marketers exploiting opportunities that arise? On the whole, there is an element of luck involved. Anyone producing a cricketing title in the UK this summer experienced a huge surge of interest as Britain won the Ashes for the first time in 18 years. That could not have been predicted. Hoped for, yes, but not predicted.

On the other hand, it is human nature to look for patterns, and it is definitely possible to tune into the patterns of behaviour and guess the direction that popular opinion is heading.

A good publisher can spot trends and market needs. Whilst there are many stories about great manuscripts being turned down by publishers who didn't spot the market potential, there are many stories that prove publishers can also accurately identify what the market is looking for:

- Louisa May Alcott was advised, after many attempts at publication, "Stick to your teaching; you can't write." Her first self-publication of poetry in 1851 was followed by the publication of many short stories and poems in magazines. Finally, on the advice of a publisher, she wrote *Little Women* – a story about American life from a girl's perspective to compete with the very popular Oliver Optic books for boys. By 1870 she was a best-selling author.
- Arthur Conan Doyle sold the rights to *A Study in Scarlett,* a novel that marked the debut of Sherlock Holmes and received a derisory £25 for it. However, a Philadelphia editor saw it, recognised its potential and commissioned Doyle to write another 'Sherlock Holmes' story, which marked the beginning of a long career.

Many authors advise me that they wrote their manuscript because they personally had needed the information and couldn't find it... ergo, if they needed it then there must be other people out there who are also searching for it. This is, in itself, a form of trend predicting.

In summary, the answer is yes – people can predict trends and jump onto fashion bandwagons. The skill is in getting there first, and mainstream publishing tends to work on very long lead times. In this respect, self-publishers hold the advantage.

Self-publishers can react faster to trends

"But... who is the arbiter of what's good or not; or what's going to sell or not?"

Another critical question facing the 'rejected' author is whether the rejection is down to the fact that they simply cannot write, or the publisher simply cannot see the opportunity.

The publishers are the first to admit that some great works slip through the net. There are many examples throughout publishing history where some of our most admired authors and literary masterpieces have been rejected in one way or another:

- Agatha Christie was many times rejected before The Bodley Head agreed to publish *The Mysterious Affair at Styles* after sitting on it for 18 months. She then went on to write a further ninety titles! Not bad for a rejected author.
- William Golding's *Lord of the Flies* (first written as Strangers from Within) was rejected by 21 publishing houses before a young editor at Faber & Faber spotted its potential. After considerable changes it was published, and gradually earned him his literary reputation.
- Since his first submissions in 1900, James Joyce's work was systematically rejected for his works *The Dubliners, The Portrait of an Artist as a Young Man* (serialised successfully in magazine form) and *Ulysses*, until finally in 1922 Sylvia Beach (owner of the Shakespeare & Co bookshop in Paris) published *Ulysses* as a banned book. This catapulted him to fame.
- Thomas Hardy fought a long, hard battle for recognition. His first two books (*The Poor Man and the Lady* and *Desperate Remedies*) were both offered 'subsidised'

publishing deals. Hardy rejected the first offer for *The Poor Man,* but accepted and paid for *Desperate Remedies,* which sold only 370 of the 500 published. Finally, it was the serialisation of *A Pair of Blue Eyes* that brought him to the attention of a critic who commissioned him to write a serialisation for The Cornhill Magazine. He submitted the 12-part *Far from the Madding Crowd…*

- Somerset Maugham, F Scott Fitzgerald, George Orwell and John Steinbeck all received copious rejections before finally achieving publication, often times on their third, fourth or fifth novel.
- George Bernard Shaw received a steady stream of rejections for his books, articles and stories, frequently being advised to leave journalism altogether. After 5 years of relentless writing and rejection, To-Day Magazine finally published *An Unsocial Socialist* as a serialisation without payment to the author. This put his name in the public and thus launched his career. GB Shaw's last word on publishers is:

"The one service publishers have done me is to teach me to do without them. They combine commercial rascality with artistic touchiness and pettishness, without being either good businessmen or fine judges of literature. All that is necessary to the production of a book is an author and a bookseller, without any intermediate parasite." George Bernard Shaw

The fact is, publishers cannot always tell what will be successful or not. The determined author will take rejection in his stride; he will garner opinion from a wide area to assess the skill of his work and will self-publish his book to test the market.

The reader is the arbiter of what sells or not

SUMMARY

Having a literary agent still remains the Holy Grail of the publishing industry but it is nigh on impossible to get one. You can invest so much time and effort in following submission guidelines and selling yourself, or you can self-publish and encourage them to come to you.

The conglomerates excel at scale and global reach but increasingly rely on mass-market titles, and a risky strategy of one-shot, one season.

Authors may be better off seeking a longer term, more nurturing approach which the independent publishers can offer.

Ultimately, authors don't really have a choice and given half a chance, wouldn't discriminate. But few get given a chance at all.

Growing slush piles prove that submissions are a waste of time and energy. There is too little information about who is looking for what, and there is too slim a chance of being found – or authors finding the right person. Instead of sending off hundreds of submissions, instead invest time in finding out who that one person is.

Authors are better off spending their time, energy and money on perfecting their text, getting endorsement from editors and credible spokes-people. Self-publishing helps you to get your book in front of those spokes-people. Use the wealth of services available today to perfect your work and publish it to test your market.

Don't fall at the first fence; use it as the opportunity to run towards the next. Know when to accept rejection, and when not.

Understand and exploit your commercial worth; watch trends and look for information gaps. Know why you have written your book and make sure you are saying something different.

Further reading

This Book is Unpublishable by Elaine Boorish
ISBN 1-588320-47-2
This book delves into the stories of forty authors of the past whose works, although initially rejected, are today very much alive. Their experiences of repudiation can only cheer and support readers. They illustrate the need to stubbornly persist toward the goal of publication. Fortunately for English literature, many beloved and respected writers persisted despite rejections of benighted publishers. Authors featured include: Jane Austen, Charlotte Bronte, Agatha Christie, George Orwell and Beatrix Potter.

PART III

WHY WOULD YOU SELF-PUBLISH?

The purpose of this chapter is to look at the many routes to self-publishing, and what other successfully self-published authors have experienced, where the pitfalls lie and what they advise to authors setting out on a self-publishing journey.

WHAT IS SELF-PUBLISHING?

Self-publishing is when the author pays for the publication of his book. It has been called a variety of names and receives some very mixed reactions. In the UK we are constantly warned against paying for publication whereas America and Asia are celebrating the explosion of self-expression,

If you take this criticism to heart, then you will find yourself at a brick wall with nowhere to go. The determined author is best advised to know what it is he wants, what he needs and then who to approach in order to get it.

There are a number of companies operating under a number of different descriptions, the main one being simply "Self publishing" as this, after all, is what they are helping you to do. It is, in effect, an abbreviated way of saying "Self-financed publishing" but the fact is…

The end-reader doesn't care who paid for the publication; they just want to know if the book's any good!

Below are some of the descriptions, and what they mean.

Independent self-publishing

Independent self-publishing is when the author buys in incremental services as he needs them and project manages the whole process of publication. This activity could be defined as:

"The author retains control over his book at all stages of the production process ie what text style to use, the cover design, the cover price, the book's size, format and layout, the number of copies printed, distribution methods and marketing spend. The author retains the copyright to that work, which is important if he wants to try and sell his book on to a commercial publisher at a future date".

In summary, a self-published author is the author who has taken control of the many aspects to publishing in order to get his book out there. He may buy in certain services on a fee basis, for example: editing and proof-reading to typesetting and printing services, but he ultimately owns all the rights (copyright and royalties) to the text until such time as he trades rights to make sales.

This is fine in principle. In practice, not many authors actually *know* what they are looking for and for this reason it is important to understand the publishing process and industry standard practices. Publishing is a many-skilled process, and some people adapt better to being a jack-of-all trades. To help you determine if this is the right route for you, I have thoroughly explored it in PART IV: Independent Self-publishing, pointing out tips, advice and guidelines and concluding with a summary of the main findings.

Self-publishing services companies

There are many reasons why you might decide to work with a self-publishing company. Maybe you prefer to focus on the parts of the process you are good at; maybe you are holding down a full time job or career (this includes mothers raising a family!) and simply cannot undertake the whole process yourself.

Therefore you may want to consider approaching a self-publishing services company. They offer a wide range of services between them and many have proven track records, which is obviously what you are looking for. The confusion arises as the companies describe themselves differently and offer varying different services – how does an author begin to choose the right one? Descriptions you may have heard of include self-publishers, subsidy / partnership / joint venture publishers or print-on-demand. There is no hard and fast definition, but essentially this activity can be described as:

"A company with access to editors, typesetters, designers and printers to produce a credible and quality publication; they project manage the publishing process on behalf of an author against a specific and pre-agreed contract."

Some companies offer a fuller, more comprehensive publishing service that goes beyond simply a typesetting/ formatting exercise, producing books under their own imprint and offering a raft of post-production activities such as reprinting, warehousing, distribution and fulfilment. For ease of reference later on in the book, I have called them Full Service Self-publishing Companies.

Other companies offer a range of services that culminate in the production of your book as a print-on-demand title. The principle of print-on-demand is analysed on pages 181 to 188, and companies offering a print-on-demand publishing service are investigated more fully in Part V: POD Publishers.

To help you decide what type of service may be of most use to you, I have carried out a full evaluation of Self-Publishing Services Companies in Part V. This section is punctuated with price structures, tips, hints and guidelines to help authors get the most out of working with these companies, and culminates in an analysis of Advice and Guidance.

Partnership publishing

This is a new term that has crept into the market recently, and is an alternative way of expressing the self-publishing author who works with a self-publishing services company, using their skills and expertise and ultimately printing under their imprint.

Some of these companies or imprints may also share in the financial risks of the venture, but they decide which ones they will invite as they are acting like mainstream publishing houses and staking their own reputations on the viability of the text. Because they are staking their reputation on the viability of the text, they usually require greater input and say on the final production.

There are currently only three companies offering this – Pen Press (under the *Indepenpress* imprint); Matador and The Book Guild, who offer a range of 'partnership' contracts under the descriptions of Commissioned or Co-operative Publishing.

"Vanity" publishing

Vanity publishing was a term coined in the Sixties for companies who praise the high quality of a manuscript and charge a high figure for publishing it. Other terms such as subsidy and joint venture came along during the Seventies and Eighties. There is a fuller investigation about vanity publishing (see section on "Who are the Cowboys" on page 265).

It is easy to be alarmed and many of the warnings will ring in the ears of authors that have gone with a self-publishing services company, leaving you fearing that you have been hood-winked.

Authors should be cautious and should absolutely know what they are signing up to. You should arm yourself with information – understand the publishing process, know what you are buying, know your role in the process and exactly what you should expect to receive at the end.

You should own 100% of royalties up to delivery of books. If you then use the services of a company to sell your books, then you should expect to assign pre-agreed royalties to them to pay for this service.

Given that there are so many companies offering a good, reliable and honest service, many of the rogue 'vanity' publishers have gone out of business. The message remains that authors must be informed in order to avoid these rogue traders. Equally, as the self-publishing industry co-ordinates itself and sets standards, any rogue traders will be squeezed out as they only bring down the reputation of the self-publishing business.

"Production financed" agreements

Production-financed agreements are an age-old tradition in publishing, and have recently been relaunched by Macmillan under the name "New Writing".

The Macmillan New Writing Scheme offers a no-advance, standardised terms contract for first time authors. Books are put through a streamlined publishing process, and published in a series format – cloth hard-back with designed dust-jacket and a quality paper inside. The quality of the writing has to be good at the outset, so there is minimal editing, and the book is launched to the trade through the standard Macmillan distribution and sales channels, although individual title marketing will be minimal. The book price is circa £15.00 and authors will receive a higher than average royalty of 20%. Using POD technology, the book will remain in print for 2 years irrespective of sales.

In the past, self-publishing could be undertaken by a recognised publishing house under the agreement that the author would underwrite the costs of production. The publisher may have recommended this route because he couldn't see the merit in the book and was therefore to risk his hard-earned profit margin on certain titles, he may have still been prepared to put his "reputation" on a new title ie. put his logo on the spine without any financial risk to himself.

Macmillan's New Writing Agreement is really a resurrection of this activity, yet it has caused a wide-range of reaction. Some publishers agree that there is viability in this route, whilst some authors have expressed dissent, criticising the scheme as being "*the Ryannair of publishing*" or like "*putting a bet on every horse in the race, without paying for the bets*". Some literary agents were sceptical of Macmillan's motives, although Michael Barnard of Macmillan was quick to reassure that they will continue to acquire most of their titles through agents. The New Writing offer is merely an additional initiative, and it is worth noting that since the launch of the scheme that only 8 contracts have been signed to date (Sept 05).

The loudest dissent came from The Guardian as Robert McCrum stated that the *"days of taste and literary discrimination at Macmillan are over"* which Barnard countered, saying *"It's about time the publishing industry owned up to the fact that there are tens of thousands of good new writers that don't get published. It was Macmillan's sponsorship of the Richard & Judy New Writing competition that demonstrated how some great authors just get lost in the ether."*

Whichever way you look at it, what this chiefly shows is the degree of change in the market at a fundamental level. *"It demonstrates the dismal editorial conditions prevailing and the desperation and pressures under which they are forced to work. The sums of money expended on new books have become unsustainable as marketing departments exercise the bigger judgements over and above the editorial departments. Macmillan's initiative is a telling commentary on an industry hovering on the brink of crisis." (Robert McCrum, Guardian Unlimited, 15/5/2005)*

Time will tell.

Whichever route you choose to follow, you are ultimately self-publishing. Following the old adage, "If you want something doing, do it yourself", self-publishing is an obvious route. It comes into its own as a desirable route when authors know exactly what they want and why they want it.

THE SELF-PUBLISHER'S HALL OF FAME

History demonstrates that hundreds of authors have self-published since the beginning of book printing. In fact, private printing used to be the pinnacle of publishing rather than being dismissed as mere vanity.

People continue to write, and never more voraciously than an Englishman, so a Portuguese colleague told me recently. The English love the written word, which is why Britain has such a fantastic literary reputation today.

We won't lie down and meekly accept rejection; we have always searched for other avenues to publish our crafted word, our story or our message. Today we see a steady stream of new authors and new publishers as the modern day author is spoiled for choice as to how he will write, publish, promote and sell his text. Self-publishing is poised to become the standard route to publication as authors can pick and choose which medium best suits their needs.

Andy Warhol predicted that we would all have our five minutes of fame, and with self-publishing, internet blogs, e-publishing, podcasting etc this is increasingly likely. It may be to an increasingly smaller audience, but the worldwide web will help us find our readers and enable our readers to find the text they wish to read.

Successful self-published authors from the past

Many of our biggest literary names have, at some point, paid for the production of their early works, sometimes INCLUDING the works they are most famous for. Some of the below are examined more closely further on; in the meantime, below is a summary list Hall of Fame – some names will surprise you!

- Jane Austen underwrote the production costs of *Sense & Sensibility*
- J M Barrie self-published *Better Dead* following rejection of his book *A Child of Nature*.
- L Frank Baum self-published *Father Goose* and used the profits to self-publish *The Wonderful Wizard of Oz*.
- A E Houseman's *A Shropshire Lad* was rejected by publishers before being published by Kegan Paul at the poet's own expense.
- Edward Lear self-financed the production of his third edition of *A Book of Nonsense* when Routledge refused to publish it.
- Charlotte and her sisters agreed to bear the production costs for two of their three titles (*Wuthering Heights* and *Agnes Grey* - Charlotte's *The Professor* having been rejected). Two months later, Charlotte submitted *Jane Eyre* which was published under contract within 6 weeks. Her sisters' two books were then published on the back of this success.
- Leo Tolstoy paid 4,500 roubles for the first printing of *War and Peace* – one of the greatest novels of world literature
- Marcel Proust self-published the first 1500 pages of his greatest work *Remembrance of Things Past.* His work is considered among the greatest works of modern literature
- Mark Twain self-published *Huckleberry Finn* when he tired of the foolishness of his publishers. He then re-invested his money to invent one of the first working typewriters
- Walt Whitman self-published *Leaves of Grass*
- Hugh Hefner self-published the first edition of *Playboy* magazine

The list of authors who self-published their first novel/s is endless, and it is undoubtedly their self-belief and determination which contributed to people becoming aware of them and their future success in publishing. ...

- Alexandre Dumas, author of *Three Musketeers* and *Count of Monte Cristo*, self-published his first books
- George Bernard Shaw was a jobbing printer who self-published his first works before writing *Pygmalion* and *St Joan*. In 1925 he won the Nobel Prize for Literature.
- Edgar Rice Burroughs self-published some of his first books before writing *Tarzan*

The list is endless - Alfred, Lord Tennyson, George Gordon (Lord Byron), Percy Bysshe Shelley, Thomas Hardy, T S Eliot, Virginia Woolf, Edgar Allan Poe, Elizabeth Barratt Browning, Ernest Hemingway, D H Lawrence, William Blake, Laurence Sterne, Rudyard Kipling, Anais Nin, Zane Grey, Ezra Pound, Alexander Pope, Gertrude Stein... and undoubtedly many more.

Even if they didn't self-publish, the rejections still came thick and fast. It was only the most resilient that made it through. However, what history can't reveal is how many authors struggled vainly on without achieving their goals – possibly running themselves into bankruptcy whilst chasing their dream.

**Resilience is important;
knowing when to stop is critical.**

More recently, we have examples of authors self-publishing in order to get their foot in the door, and achieving great success:

- Graham Taylor self-published *Shadowmancer* in 2002. He sold US rights a year later for half a million dollars and has sold film rights for $6.8m for this & *Wormwood*.

- *A Year in the Merde* by Stephen Clarke; sold 3000 copies and got a deal with Bantam Press.
- *Mokee Joe* by Pete Murray; first published by Pen Press and sold 12,000; Hodder Children's then acquired rights for a 3-book deal and a film deal is in the offing.
- *The Pocket Book of Patriotism* by George Courtauld sold 37,500 in the first few months before being picked up by Halstead Books. In total he has sold 250,000, although only 105,000 have gone through the tills. The rest have been through the website.
- *The Zartarbia Tales* by Ana Fischel; sold 7,000 in first quarter of launch; became a Borders no. 3 bestseller, scooping reviews across all children's media. The launch of her second book has attracted the attentions of Hollywood.
- Mike Gerber self-published *Barry Trotter* before selling the rights for several hundred thousand dollars.
- *Contest* by Matthew Reilly successfully self-published; since then, he has published *Ice Station* and *Temple*, the former being sold in 12 countries and bidding at Frankfurt Book Fair hit $600,000; Movie rights to *Ice Station* have since been sold to Paramount.
- *Alfie's Adventures* by Gerald Howe; sold 160,000 to Virgin Airlines Kids packs.
- *Gypsy Masala* by Preethi Nair; she was short-listed for Publicist of the Year after self-publicising.
- *The Art of Falling* by Deborah Lawrenson first published by Matador and sold to Arrow Books.
- Roddy Doyle's first novel, *The Commitments*, was self-published in 1987 to much critical praise. This story of a working-class Irish band put together by young Jimmy Rabbitte "committed to bringing soul to Ireland" was adapted into a hit movie in 1991.

- *Legally Blonde* by Amanda Brown; used First Books to publish as a POD book; now a major film starring Reese Witherspoon
- *Cold Mountain* by Charles Frazier was self-published; sales recently hit $1.6 million in its 57th week on *The New York Times* bestseller list.
- Viggo Mortensen set up Perceval Press, direct mailing a 20-title list including his own books
- Will Clarke's *Lord Vishnu's Love Handles* – currently being filmed by Paramount
- *Two Kinds of Silence* by Mark Blayney; won the Somerset Maugham award
- *The Dice Man* by Luke Reinhart; this success spawned many subsequent titles
- *To the End of the World* by Colin Foreman
- *The Promised One* by David Alric, distributed via the very difficult to penetrate WH Smiths.
- Jill Paton Walsh, established children's author, self-published *Knowledge of Angels;* short-listed for the 1994 Booker Prize
- Timothy Mo was dissatisfied with his publisher's offer for his new novel, and self-published *Brownout on Breadfruit* (1996)
- J L Carr's *A Month in the Country* (1980) was twice short-listed for the Booker Prize. Carr had seven novels published in the conventional way, but as well as writing fiction, the ex-headmaster self-published a series of handy 16 page booklets featuring the work of poets and miscellaneous figures from sport and history.
- Christopher Paolini published *Eragon* with the help of his parents; sold rights in a deal worth $0.5m.
- *The Key to Chintak: The Zamorian Chronicles* by John Howard, self-published by Antony Rowe

- *It so Happens* by Patricia Ferguson; short-listed for the Orange Prize.
- *Princess Poppy's Party* and *Saffron's Wedding* by Janey Jones; sold 25,000 and got a deal with Walker Books
- *Long March to Freedom* by Tom Hargrove
- Margaret Atwood: first volume of poetry *Double Persephone* in 1961
- Hilary Bradt self-published her first award-winning guidebook
- Susan Hill has been successfully self-publishing her books out of a Cotswold barn
- Stephen King was the first novelist to self-publish a novel via a serialised format on the Internet; more than half a million people viewed the novel

Not to forget in music…

- Herb Alpert & Jeremy Moss started A&M Records with $100 each in 1962 and sold it for $500m to Polygram in 1989. Not bad, either!

On the strength of this list of self-publishing successes, why leave the manuscript gathering dust on the top shelf? Pick up your courage and every spare ounce of energy and do it!

Write because you have something to say
Self-publish because you can afford to!

"But... the publishing and bookselling industry operates so many closed doors to self-published titles."

In the past, self-publishing has suffered from rogue printers posing as publishers, producing woefully inadequate books whilst charging excessive fees. It has left booksellers wary of such 'vanity' titles that they can't sell. There are many reservations, closed doors and glass ceilings towards self-published books for a host of reasons:

- Too many self-published titles are badly written and just not interesting
- They glut an already over-supplied market, creating too much 'noise' and preventing consumers from finding the quality material
- They are increasingly better-produced, looking good on the outside but not delivering on the inside; this causes consumer confusion as they can no longer judge a book by its cover
- They clog the system, supplying poor quality information to the computerised databases. Booksellers complain they frequently waste time hunting for books that don't show up on the systems.

But the tide is turning. Whilst I still encounter reticence on occasion, opinion is changing. Over the last year, whilst researching this book, I have spoken to people who admitted they had always been distinctly anti "vanity" published titles but could see the change in the quality of these titles. They acknowledged the winds of change, and that increasingly more self-published titles were achieving literary and marketable standards.

As the quality of material and production values improve, it is increasingly difficult to differentiate a self-publishing title from a mainstream title. In fact, some mass-market paperbacks are distinctly shoddier, with poor typesetting, inconsistently cut pages so text is wonky or too close to the edge. My pet hate is the excessive use of broken words and the reliance of the hyphen. Yet these practices seem to be infiltrating the market, and arguably the average self-published title is better produced.

Even as recently as two years ago, there was greater resistance to self-published titles but the real demonstration of change came during a conversation with Borders recently. When I explained a certain title I wanted them to stock was self-published, the store manager looked pleased and said they were experiencing a lot of sales with many self-published titles they had chosen to stock. Hooray! Somebody, somewhere finally seeing the merit!

The word of warning to self-publishing authors is to ensure they produce work of quality. Any authors seeking publishing services has always been, and will always be, that they gain independent endorsement about the quality of their writing and their story, and buy publishing services from individuals or companies who are qualified to provide them.

Before you shout out the battle-cry of **"I'll self-publish! I'll do it for myself!!"** stop to think whether you can do all of this by yourself? How time consuming is it, or do you need more than 24 hours in a day? Have you the necessary skill and expertise, or do you know people who you can reliably pay to do parts of it on your behalf? How steep is the learning curve? Will it provide any financial return? What do the successfully self-published authors say?

WHAT THE SUCCESSFULLY SELF-PUBLISHED AUTHORS SAY...

The stories of the successful self-published authors paint a varied and fascinating picture. No two experiences of self-publishing are the same and they have all learned different lessons along the way. Here, they share their experiences and offer their tips and advice.

G P Taylor

Author of *Shadowmancer, Wormwood* and *Tersias*

Original edition
Mount Publishing 2002

Faber & Faber edition
2003

Graham Taylor was 42 years old when he decided to seize the moment to self-publish. Much as he'd always wanted to write and had a fascination with 19th century history, he was a novice at writing and hadn't researched or planned the story out when he sat down to write it regardless. *Shadowmancer* was born. Despite being told by an online editor that the story was poor, Graham successfully sold 2500 copies in four weeks and had signed with Faber & Faber by the fifth week. To capitalise on such an unprecedented start, *Shadowmancer* jumped to number 1 for 15 weeks after Faber & Faber re-released it.

Did you understand anything about publishing prior to starting, or was it a very steep learning curve?
It was a very steep learning curve as I knew nothing about publishing. Having researched the market, I paid a printer in Finland £3,500 to produce 2000 copies of the book. There are 304 pages and printers in the UK were charging double.

What mistakes did you make?
The biggest mistake was on pricing the book. I thought that more than doubling print costs would see me right, but I hadn't factored in all the millions of incremental costs and the huge demands on my time.

Was there ever a low-point?
The real low-point was tolerating the mountains of books and packing materials on the dining table, and the endless trips to the post office. It sounds trite, but it dominated my life and I hadn't factored any of this into my financial calculations which made it all the more frustrating.

Prior to the Faber & Faber deal, how much publicity did you undertake?
It all happened pretty quickly. Other than local bookshops and media, I didn't get a chance to go to the next level. But my advice to self-publishing authors is to start local. The nationals and chains only want to know once you have met with success at a local level. They believe that if you can't manage at a local level, you won't achieve it at a national level.

How did you get the book deal?
Ah… that was a contact. Someone I know passed the book to a former director of a major publisher; from there it went to Faber & Faber and I signed. It was pretty quick, but because of my early success with the title and that I proved I had an audience, I also negotiated a good percentage – better than the average first-timer.

How did you get the first national reviews?
That was the Faber & Faber media machine. It was that first article in The Telegraph that really made the difference to sales. Not all reviews work, but a sizeable feature definitely does.

How does the experience of being a self-published author compare to being a published author?
Faber & Faber are a great company to work with, and they have definitely made the difference in terms of distribution and promotional or sales deals. That's the central element a publishing house brings to an author that an author cannot do by themselves.
The one negative is the loss of control. You've basically handed the baby to the nanny, and the author's role becomes purely publicity. It's slightly harder to take when you've been personally overseeing every part of the process and hand-posting each book that's ordered. I think I'd get Kim Cross at Grosvenor Publishing to do all that for me now

Would you do it again completely independently, or would you use a self-publishing services company?
I would definitely do it again independently. I have no experience of self-publishing services companies so can't say if I would use them. But I learned a lot the first time round, and would certainly do it again.

Do you remain very involved in the marketing?
Yes. It's the only way to sell both the book and yourself as an author.

Do you think the internet plays a role in building an author's reputation and/or expanding awareness of the book?
It certainly plays a role, but it can build you up as soon as knock you down.

What do you foresee as some of the major changes in the publishing industry in the near future?
I think that self-publishing is definitely going to become increasingly more commonplace, and that literary agents / publishers will look to self-published titles to find new authors. Why not? It's a perfect testing ground. And despite the online editor saying my work was rubbish, Faber & Faber did not change a single word of my book when they took it on and published it. Three books later and a film deal doesn't say to me that my writing's rubbish!

Other changes…
I think we will lose a major retailer at some point. It's not sustainable with the current plethora of major booksellers, and I suspect it will be a company with a very centralised buying and promotions policy. Limiting core stock and focussing on mass-market is contrary to market needs. Companies like Ottakar's still hand-sell; their staff love books, they

read books and know about books. They are a real bookshop, and this, I believe, will stand them in good stead through this period of change. I do worry that they will be bought out by another major chain and turned into a book selling version of Tesco.

What advice would you give a self-publishing author?
That's easy...

- PR, PR, PR... launch local then build
- Print cheaply
- Expect to make no money and don't give up the day job. You just have to make the publishing project fit in around the job that pays you.

Stephen Clarke (Paul West)

Author of *A Year in the Merde, Merde Actually, Beam Me Up* and *Who Killed Beano*?

Original edition
Red Garage Books 2004

Black Swan edition
2005

I understand you had been trying to become a published writer for ages. Why the pseudonym, or rather why hide the fact you were self-publishing?
I thought that people would be prejudiced against self-published authors (can't get themselves published, therefore must be unpublishable). So I decided to create my punky, anti-establishment publishers and announce that we'd found these great, new authors who were all too worthy of publication. I took my three novels as my publisher's stable of authors. I claimed one as my own; *A Year in the Merde* as the autobiography of Paul West; and Chris Kent, the author of *Who Killed Beano?* was my female author. But, I thought, what if someone wants to interview her? Am I going to put on a falsetto voice and insist on phone interview only? Non! So the poor girl had to die, as her author bio says "in a mysterious diving accident in the south of France".

How much publicity did you undertake? What form did it take?
I decided to deal with one book at a time, starting with *A Year in the Merde.* I wrote press releases which I produced just as professionally as the books (I have experience of writing press releases because of my day job as a magazine editor). I sent them to every book reviewer in the UK daily and Sunday press, plus some contacts in the French press as I live in Paris. At first nothing happened; I was ignored - Red Garage Books was totally unknown. But then one journalist from the

French version of the free daily, *Metro*, called me saying she'd got the book and was reading it (slowly as it was in English). I picked up hope and kept calling her up to ask how she was getting along, and eventually she wrote a piece, and it all took off from there. The effect of one article in the press can be quite amazing.

How long did it take for sales to start taking off?
I sold practically none for the first three months from 1 April 2004, then the *Metro* article came out and I was selling literally a thousand a week.

What is the most impactful piece of marketing you did?
I guess sending out all the press releases, but ultimately it was securing just the one favourable write-up. Once one writer has mentioned you, others jump on the bandwagon. All it takes is one good article.

Would you do it again completely independently, or would you use a self-publishing services company?
Independently, IF you are like me and have a bit of experience with editing, copy-reading, etc. I didn't need a self publishing company once I'd found a printer (a friend of a friend) and a layout designer (another friend). If you're crap at grammar, and don't have friends who can re-read your stuff and tell you where you're going wrong, you need an editor.

How does the experience of being a self-published author compare to being a published author, now you are with Bantam? Or is this (i) too early days or (ii) indiscreet?
The funny thing is that Bantam still ask me to write my own back cover blurbs. Whether that's just because I've done it before with some success, I don't know. Maybe Dan Brown has to write his own blurbs too.
The best thing about having a publisher is you don't have to deliver the books yourself, or go and buy loads of jiffy bags and then lug them to the post office. The worst thing is, you only get 10% royalties.

Do you remain very involved in the marketing?
Yes, and I also have input on press releases.

How steep was the learning curve, and was there any information out there?
Very, very steep. I muddled through, and somehow seemed to have got a lot of things right. But then, I have worked for a publisher before; whilst I didn't use those contacts at all, I knew how a book is put together. Basically, all I tried to do was make books that look exactly like "real" publisher's books, to put myself on the same playing field as them.

How much do you think it cost you up to launch?
I decided I had £3000 to spend and spent it all.

What advice would you give a self-publishing author?
Go for it. You have nothing to lose, except whatever money you're prepared to put in to it and even then it's better spent than sending huge manuscripts out to publishers and agents who won't read them.

Preethi Nair

Author of *Gypsy Masala, The Colour of Love* and *100 Shades of White*

The original edition
Ninefish 2000

HarperCollins
Edition 2004

Preethi wrote and self-published *Gypsy Masala*, then set herself up as publicist Pru Menon to hype up the book before launch. To do this, she 'gave up the day job' and dedicated herself to launching her title. Despite several print disasters, a non-existent distribution channel and a fuel crisis, she got the book into the shops and public consciousness. HarperCollins have now signed her and have since released a number of titles, one of which is being made into a two part drama by the BBC.

She won the Asian Woman of Achievement award for her endeavours and was also short listed as Publicist of the Year for the PPC awards.

Preethi says that it was a rollercoaster of a journey... very, very tough. *"Every time I made some sort of breakthrough, like getting my books stocked at the distributors or shops or getting press etc, something would then happen to make me question the whole thing - pages missing, books being incorrectly bound then having to deal with the returns. I went from emotional high to real low, and so many times I felt like giving up."*

How much publicity did you undertake (either as Pru or Preethi)? What form did it take? ie. Phone calls, press releases, fairs, booksignings, promotional materials etc.

All of the above. I wrote a targeted press release according to who I was sending the book to, sent out hundreds of copies of *Gypsy Masala* and followed it up with calls. I began hyping my book six months in advance of publication date, and I completely immersed myself in the publishing world. I attended other people's book launches in an attempt to make contacts and visited hundreds of book shops.

How many books were you selling per month approx in first 3 months of launch?
In most stores where I was stocked, it was a steady trickle of sales ie. 300 copies, but in one shop alone it sold 2,000 copies in the first 3 months, and I think it was this that made the difference. They got completely behind the book by doing a lovely display which really boosted sales and it is this that puts you on the radar of the major chains and other publishers.

When did you finally 'come clean' that Preethi the author and Pru the publicist were one and the same person?
When journalists found out I was Pru the PR girl and that NineFish was my publishing company.

How/when did you get first national reviews?
National reviews only began appearing when I signed with HarperCollins and my first book with them *One Hundred Shades of White* came out.

How long did it take?
In total 2 years.

Do you remain very involved in the marketing?
I do in the sense that I proactively promote the title that I am working on. Publishers have a limited resource and the PR machinery is working on at last 10 other titles a month, so it's important to be proactive if you want a wide readership.

What, in your opinion, was the most impactful activity you undertook that yielded the most response – either from media, booksellers or sales?
Visiting bookshops individually. The one bookshop where it sold 2,000 copies was because I had visited them and they had made *Gypsy Masala* staff choice.

How does the experience of being a self-published author compare to being a published author?
It doesn't compare on any level. When I was self publishing, I had a triple life, I had to do everything myself, there was no time to write. Now, I have time to write, but I miss all the chaos and activity.

Would you do it again completely independently, or would you use a self-publishing services company?
I have a lot of experience now and so if I were to do it again, it would be independently.

What advice would you give a self-publishing author?
Don't do it! No, don't do it unless you are 100% committed. Be very focussed. Think of what you are doing it for, expect failure and rejection, but have commitment and faith in your work.

Gerald Howe

Author of the *Alfie's Adventures* series

Why did you decide to self-publish?

I tried unsuccessfully to get a publisher interested, but it was often evident that my manuscript was merely being transferred to my self-addressed envelope and returned. Finally I decided it wasn't worth the effort as I rarely even got a response.

It seemed like a classic chicken and egg situation, but I wasn't going to be beaten(!). I had taken the trouble to write the book and, even if it never reached the mainstream market, I thought it would be nice to have a few stories to read to my grandchildren (if, as and when...). I felt that part of the problem was, by simply submitting a manuscript, they couldn't see the potential of how I envisaged my book.

So I did my research and decided to self-publish, ultimately choosing to work with a self-publishing company as I am an entrepreneur with all the time limitations that brings.

What was your experience?

I chose a company that I figured I could do business with; and this proved right. Pen Press did what they said they would do – designed a great cover, edited and delivered a good-looking book in the promised time frame for the agreed budget.

What were you hoping for in the beginning?

I never expected it to be a best seller, I just wanted to justify the expense of the printing! The radio and television interviews were a bonus, as was the book signing at the local Ottakars. I felt very rewarded personally by the experience of actually meeting one's customers and talking through my product.

One of the most encouraging responses that I got was from a group of 11 year old schoolboys that I read to who were really interested and enthusiastic – and I thought they said kids were disengaged nowadays? They were the ones who inspired me to write Alfie as a series, rather than as a one-off book.

What, in your opinion, was the most impactful activity you undertook that yielded the most response – either from media, booksellers or sales?

The pleasant surprise in the tale is after the first launch, when we re-edited and re-designed *Alfie's Adventures* to include illustrations, in response to a marketing idea. We then relaunched *Alfie's Adventures* to great success as we secured a deal with Virgin - this was undeniably the most impactful activity.

How did you secure the Virgin Airlines deal?

It was one of my bright ideas that an airline might be interested in putting *Alfie's Adventures* into their Kids packs. I chose Virgin because I like them, and sent a copy off to them. Following a successful meeting with the Virgin buyers, they put it forward for consideration, but after a month, they came back and said that they liked the book, but the decision had been put on ice. So I thought that was the end of things.

Soon afterwards, I stood in a bookshop studying the children's shelves, and I realized that what I thought was fantastic actually lacked "something" to make it stand out from the crowd. So I engaged an illustrator who clearly had the ability to sum up a chapter fairly humorously in one picture; Tony from Channimation then drew eighteen illustrations for my first book, whilst I wrote Books 2, 3 and 4.

We re-approched Virgin with a much better product and a series concept. The response was excellent, but then the real work began – book formats, weights (obviously paramount for airlines), quantities, drop-loads, freight, price, deadlines etc. Pen Press were terrific in liaising with the buyers to get the deal done, and after eighteen months of work we recently delivered the first 80,000 of Alfie's Adventures Books 1 and 2 to Hong Kong.

I am hoping that with this kind of circulation that the books will be popular and, having written books three and four, that a market will be created for my books.

Would you do it differently next time?
Why? Working with a self-publishing services company is invaluable when you are a complete novice. I'm a good businessman, but don't know anything about publishing. I really needed guidance and input to make the books the success they have become so far. We have been a true partnership.

What advice would you give a self-publishing author?
My advice? People should view self-publishing as a positive action to take to get your work published – particularly to get it published in the format and style you envisaged. It brings the whole product and concept together.

Once you have a published copy in your hand, it is up to you to decide your next steps; whether you want to put time, effort and money into making it a success. I have been approached by a potential agent after getting the Virgin deal; but equally I am happy self-publishing. I am still in control.

Deborah Lawrenson
Author of *The Art of Falling*

Original edition
Stamp Publishing 2003

Arrow edition
2005

What was your experience as a self-publisher?
I had already written three novels published by Heinemann when I became a self-publisher, and I came to it reluctantly at first, but then with a mounting sense of excitement and adventure.

For nearly five years I had been researching and writing, then trying to find a publisher for, my more literary fourth novel The Art of Falling, and it had come as a nasty shock to me that none of my previous publishing contacts wanted to know about this change of direction. A new, well-regarded London literary agent absolutely loved it, but couldn't place it after a year. The problem, she reported, was that publishers found it difficult to categorize: was it literary, or was it commercial? This was a refrain I was to hear often in the next few years… I couldn't understand why that wasn't a positive if the book also had the good qualities many admitted it did.

Then, what started as an act of daring and desperation slowly became reality. My husband and his brother were involved in a printing firm, Stamp, but it did not have any of the necessary distribution networks into bookshops. They could produce a top-quality trade paperback, but there was no point in doing it if it had to be sold out of cardboard boxes.

So I trawled the internet for such a company. Within minutes of speaking to Matador I knew that I had found someone we could do business with. He agreed to produce the book under the Stamp imprint, warehouse and distribute it. The cover was designed by

Richard Cook, the brilliant graphic artist at Stamp, and we presented Matador with exactly what we wanted.

The feeling of control was immense and exhilarating. Matador were fantastic to work with - they made it easy. Nothing went wrong. The commission was delivered on time and on budget, and, if anything the finished book looked even better than we'd hoped: a good quality, matt-cover paperback retailing for £7.99. The only glitch was at the beginning of the sales campaign when the book was not listed on one of the vital book industry databases essential for shops to order – but that was our fault at Stamp because we hadn't understood the purpose of a form Jeremy had sent us to complete. Which just goes to show how much a novice self-publisher needs the guidance of a professional.

How much publicity did you undertake? What form did it take?
Matador prepared a press release and Stamp printed 5000 advertising flyers. I contacted every local publication I could think of, as well as radio stations. Exactly what a mainstream publisher would do for an author, in other words. I also sent review copies to national newspapers.

How long did it take for sales to start taking off?
About a month after publication, I had a miraculous day. There was a review in the Daily Mail books pages – and it was an amazing one. The reviewer called it "a superbly crafted novel that deserves to be called the new Captain Corelli or perhaps the new *Birdsong*...moving, lyrical and elegiac" – and that very afternoon I was due to talk about the book on BBC Radio Kent. The review was read out several times on air, and that's when the book really started to move, both through bookshops and Amazon.

What, in your opinion, was the most impactful activity you undertook that yielded the most response?
After sending out the review copies which led to such a lucky break, I would say the steeling myself to call bookshop after bookshop asking whether they would be interested stocking the book. I then sent copies of the Mail review, and other newspaper pieces, along with the flyer with all the order details – and quite often a free copy so that fiction buyers and managers could see how good the product looked, and make up their own minds whether they rated the content.

I built up good relationships with several key bookstores where staff began to recommend the book to their regular customers and reading groups.

Would you do it again completely independently, or would you use a self-publishing services company?
I would definitely use a self-publishing services company. Even though I'd had books published before I simply didn't know enough about the logistics of production and distribution. It would be very difficult to supply bookshop orders independently, and you want to look as professional as possible.

Do you remain very involved in the marketing?
At the beginning I was completely involved. Every day I made myself do at least three things to push the book on – a morning tackling bookshops, approaches to local libraries, the media, reading groups - and was very much the driving force. After it did well enough to get noticed by Ottakar's head office, I sold the UK rights to Random House, some nine months after the Stamp edition was published. Random House has done a fantastic job of marketing the new Arrow edition of The Art of Falling, and thanks to a poster campaign and being chosen for the WHSmith Fresh Talent promotion for 2005, it's done well. Even so, I've still been independently setting up what I can myself, mainly through all the contacts I made the first time round.

There's also the rather wonderful bonus that the Stamp edition has become a collectors' item. The first copies auctioned on eBay fetched around £200 each! So I do a little wheeler-dealing with the few copies I have left in cardboard boxes...

How steep was the learning curve, and was there any information out there?
Matador did all the work a mainstream publisher would do, but with the great plus that I could make the final editorial decisions. I loved having so much control of my own work.

The steepest learning curve was the bookselling. There wasn't much help around for how to do that. I did it all by instinct.

How much do you think it cost you up to launch?
Up to launch, about £5,000. All in, including all the marketing costs, sales and distribution commissions, telephone, internet and travel, the final figure came in at around £7,000. This included a cover that cost the best part of £1,000 to design and licence the use of expensive

Getty and Hulton photographs. The good news is that, with the sales at the end to first edition collectors, I just about scraped a profit.

What advice would you give a self-publishing author?
Hire a professional editor and proof-reader. Commission the best cover you can afford and make sure the finished look is as close to a mainstream published book of the same genre as you can get it.

Before you go ahead, make sure that any company you use can supply orders efficiently direct to bookshops and the big trade distributors like Gardners and Bertrams – many large chains won't touch a book from anywhere else.

Peter Murray

Author of *Mokee Joe is Coming!*, *Mokee Joe Recharged* and *The Doomsday Trail*

Original edition
Pen Press 2003

Hodder Childrens
Edition 2004

Pete Murray made a conscious decision to self-publish from the outset as he did not want to spend time going down the route of submissions and rejections with mainstream publishers. He enlisted the help of Pen Press and paid a once only charge of £2,400 for their full publication package, which included editing and typesetting, artworking a cover designed from Murray's original painting, printing and binding an initial 100 digital review copies. These were sent out to gain endorsements, and then a first print run of 5,000 copies were run-off, complete with endorsements.

The author's local branch of Waterstone's got behind the book, creating in-store and window displays consisting of books, posters and flyers. Being a teacher, Murray also encouraged pupils to go into Waterstones to buy their signed copies, and soon other branches started to take note of the healthy sales.

A tour of schools and bookshops followed and the Mokee Joe success story had started. Pete Murray had direct access to his audience, but children (being harsh judges) would not have got behind it if the book wasn't good. The concept behind Mokee Joe was clearly a success. The author worked tirelessly, promoting his book on TV and radio interviews, and holding signing sessions, readings and talks wherever possible; all this activity well-supported by his self-publishing services partner. Just three months after the book's release, Waterstone's agreed to include it in their 'Best paperbacks of the Year'

3 for 2 Christmas promotion and Pen Press printed a further 15,000 copies – 10,000 with a unique heat sensitive colour change cover made exclusively for Waterstone's. With sales of 12,000 copies under his belt, Hodder Children's Books offered the author a three book deal and were quoted as 'on the look out for similar successfully self-published titles'.

George Courtauld
Author of The Pocket Book of Patriotism

Original edition 2004
Halstead Books Ltd

Sterling Publishing
September 2005

What was your experience?
The whole thing started off one day on a train when I observed how woefully little a group of schoolkids knew about their own history – key dates and well-known names. They lacked the 'soundbite' of history knowledge. When I got home, I discovered that there were gaps in my own children's patriotic knowledge that needed rectifying.

So I spent Christmas writing up a wallchart of dates, people, information… the stuff that any English kid should know about their history. Word spread like wildfire amongst my friends and colleagues and the wallchart, that now sat on the wall of the toilet, became hot property. I photocopied it a hundred times in a month; this is when I figured it might have a worth.

Being a headhunter, I know many people and I contacted them all in my quest to convert this concept into a publication – and so many people were willing to help. I wrote it up into a 64 page book and touted the concept around. I was told, often in no uncertain terms, that it was a stupid idea, nobody was patriotic in this country and I was wasting my time. That was when I decided I would do it myself.

How did you approach self-publishing?
I was a complete amateur and overlooked things as basic as barcodes. I had no barcode on the book – just the ISBN. I had no distribution. No accounts anywhere. Just the book – all the gear and no idea! A good friend of mine called Nick May stepped into the breach to help, and assisted in negotiating distribution etc. I am so grateful to him and all the other people who came to my aid.

In order to fund the print run, I sold my precious, precious Morgan and printed 10,000 hardback books for £11,000.

How did you sell it then?
Well, not through the bookshops. They wouldn't touch it at a national level because they "only stock books from publishers with a list of 25 or more titles" (!!). At launch, I had got the book into two independent bookshops.

The real sales came directly as a result of the launch party on 23rd November. I invited friends, business colleagues and journalists; 200 people attended and 350 copies of the book sold that night. The next morning I sold 2,500 copies and had a review in the *Daily Mail*; within the first week, I had orders of 37,500 copies! Within the first month I had sold 150,000 books.

I also created an interactive website and promoted this quite heavily. It cost me a lot of money to produce it which was risky, but essential in the absence of the book being in the bookshops. People had to be able to find me, and the web was the route in the early days.

How much did publicity play a part in the book's success?
The media is critical is building national awareness in a short time frame – and the key to success is the sudden burst of noise about a book. It builds up its own energy and momentum. After the first article appeared in the *Daily Mail* on the 24th November, the others were quick to pick it up - *The Times*, *The Telegraph*, *The Mirror*, The *Independen*t, *BBC Breakfast*, *Today Radio Five Live* and 28 other radio stations – all praising it. The Guardian dissed it completely, and on that same day, the The Labour Party Bookshop ordered 3,500 copies.

In terms of marketing budget there was none, unless you count bar drinks and lunches! In this, it is a fantastic story and I'm pleased it's my story.

Was there ever a lowpoint?
Not really – although I was sometimes taken aback by the vehemence with which some people said it was an unworkable concept in its early days. Some have since come back and admitted they were wrong.

I must confess, however, to feeling completely shell-shocked initially. It took me completely by surprise - we ran out of books and worked round the clock to fulfil the orders pouring in; the website "fell over" occasionally - we had 114,000 hits one night; I was getting thousands of letters, emails, phone calls, faxes etc every week and couldn't keep pace with it all. My wife was superb in the face of such disruption.

What made it successful in your view?
I believe a number of factors all fortuitously came together to make the book successful.

Firstly, I think *The Pocket Book of Patriotism* was successful because it made a statement. Whether you agree or disagree with the statement is immaterial; you'll buy the book anyway. People are interested in statements and opinions.

The fact that the book made a statement about patriotism also awakened the media, and the real thrust of interest came from the amount of media attention the book received. Few people could not have heard about it.

Another contributing factor was that the book sold through non-traditional outlets – schools, institutions, men's clubs etc as an educational aid or gift item. This gave it a lot of repeat purchase or bulk buy, which many books do not enjoy the luxury of. Most books are a one-off purchase, oftentimes being bought in singles rather than multiples. Whereas I sold 37,500 books online against a stock of 10,000 books.

Another contributing factor was the lack of middlemen initially – I could charge a reasonable cover price and afford to keep reinvesting the profits to reprint. I was in control of the sales; nobody could discount it so every copy sold covered both print cost and profit. I could afford to go to second print run of 50,000 copies. The fact that by the time the booksellers were ordering the books it was already heavily in demand meant that I could command Firm Sale, rather than bank-rolling stock for months on Sale/Return.

What was the most impactful activity you undertook?
Ignoring everyone and just steaming ahead and doing it!! Nobody would publish it, yet we sold 150,000 in 4 weeks. They say that the value of publishing is in subscriptions, and my book inadvertently behaved in this fashion with bulk orders and repeat orders going to institutions. There was nothing deliberate about this – however much I would like to think I had consciously engineered this.

Equally, I cannot overlook the importance of the launch party. That is what kicked it off in the beginning.

What was the biggest mistake?
Obviously not having the barcode. We sold 250,000 copies in total but only 100,000 were through the tills, which impacts on the market rating. But did it hold the book back? No, obviously not. People located it through the website and this proved to be worth its weight in gold as schools were setting up standing orders to keep a steady supply coming.

In my naivety, I hadn't realised that booksellers take such a large percentage. As a hardback book, I barely made any profit after bookseller discounts.

We weren't prepared for the stampede and this could have jeopardised those early weeks – but didn't fortunately.

What advice have you got for the self-publishing author?
Get your marketing sorted out. Understand what you are creating, why and who will want it then work like crazy to ensure the media are behind it.

Be completely prepared to push it yourself, and be prepared to deal with the media – be interviewed, go on chat shows, talk on radio etc.

George Courtauld's second book "A Pocket Book of Patriots" has been released in October by Ebury Press.

John Morrison
Author of Anthony Blair, Captain of School

I am interviewing John Morrison the week before his book launches, and we plan to follow up his experience of self-publishing in the next book.

Why did you decide to self-publish?
There are several reasons:
(i) I had done two non-fiction books before and I was frustrated by my experiences last time round. I wanted to avoid the pre-publication hell of semi-literate copy editors changing things in my book.
(ii) I wanted above all to bring the book out faster than the 18 month standard; it's a satire on Blair and he may not be around for ever.
(iii) I wanted the freedom to decide the format, design, price of the book and pick my own illustrator – and be able to commission as many illustrations as I wanted.
(iv) I also had a sneaky desire to do it just because it would be a challenge. Some people climb mountains, but I thought it would be fun if I could beat the publishers at their own game. I hope for it to provide a return, but I won't lose sleep if it doesn't.

When did you start planning it?
I started planning last November by talking to my local bookshop and Antony Rowe. Their initial estimates helped me take crucial decisions early on about price and format – hardback, in the £10-12 region, compromising slightly on the illustrations as glossy plates would have been hideously expensive.

Did you self-publish independently or with a company?
- I worked with AMOLIBROS as they offered the flexible formula I wanted where I would take the key decisions and own the books, but she would guarantee me access to a distributor. She also did

the typesetting at a very reasonable rate and offered lots of good advice, and liaison with the printers in Padstow.

- Given that I didn't know any illustrators, I ended up trawling the internet for illustration agencies, and looking through hundreds of artists' on-line portfolios to find someone with the right style. I made a shortlist of half a dozen, of whom three were interested and I paid them to do sample drawings. Finally I picked David Hopkins who had exactly the pastiche Edwardian style I was looking for.

What marketing are you doing?

- As a former Westminster journalist I have lots of contacts to draw on to get a bit of free publicity. I'm not a natural PR person and have no gift for business or selling, but I persistently badgered Sarah Crown the books editor of the Guardian Unlimited website to run extracts and finally she agreed.
- I also got extracts running in *Country Life* after sending the chapter in which young Blair goes fox hunting to Clive Aslet the editor.
- I sent out a very large number of copies to the media for review but I have no idea what results this will achieve, if any. So far I have managed to generate a number of brief newspaper stories and diary items.
- I think that one key advantage is that my book is very distinctive

How are the financial aspects going?

The final cover price of £9.99 is lower than my original estimate but should put the book in the Christmas gift price bracket, rather than up there with hardback fiction in the mid-teens price range.

I hazarded a budget of £10,000 at the outset, and have so far spent around double that - printing 5,000 hardback books, spent £6,000 on the illustrator and the rest has gone on marketing, office expenses and advertising. It's too early to say at what point I shall get my money back, as this depends on the proportion of copies bought on direct sales from the distributor by credit card.

Would you have done anything differently?

It's too early to say what I would do differently as the launch hasn't happened yet. But I am very happy at the moment that I chose the lowest possible price -- £10 is certainly a price barrier in the book trade. I'm delighted with the cover illustration which has done more to sell the book than anything else.

What's your advice to other self-publishing authors?

- Bait as many hooks as you can in all directions because you don't know which ones will nibble. Country Life would certainly not have been at the top of my list, so this was a bit of lateral thinking that paid off.
- Get going early with marketing & promotion! Start off with your ISBN and get your cover image ready, because wholesalers' monthly catalogues go to press six months before publication. Five-six months is ideal; anything less and you are struggling.
- Physically visit plenty of bookshops with the AI sheet.
- I also printed several thousand postcard flyers, which I distributed at the Labour conference and elsewhere, and lots of bookmarks for bookshops. I have advertised in one or two national magazines and on Google Adwords, and I hope this will generate traffic to my website.
- As a self-publisher, you are in the David versus Goliath business. But remember that only the top 1% of titles get any advertising and promotion at all. If you make a labour-intensive effort, making phone calls, sending emails and doing mailshots, you can ensure that your book gets more exposure than the other 99%. I got a nice interview in *Publishing News* back in June, which I copied and sent out. *The Bookseller* has taken no interest whatsoever.
- And get a good pre-publication quote from someone. I was lucky in that Matthew Parris, whom I knew very slightly, was decent enough to read the book and give me a quote. A lot of other 'names' didn't reply to my requests at all.

All of the authors interviewed above are the successful ones, if success is measured by securing mainstream contracts. But there are many other authors I have spoken to whose self-publishing endeavours did not result in a mainstream deal, a huge advance, a 3-book deal or purchase of film rights. But does this mean they failed? Not according to them:

"My book has been reviewed positively by people whose opinion I respect; it has travelled to America and been warmly received. I have met fascinating people I ordinarily wouldn't have met. All of this has made it a positive experience – and I remain optimistic that I will become an established writer in the future." Colin Campbell, author of *Through the Ruins of Midnight.*

"I secured a slot on BBC Radio Ulster, having been invited onto the show to talk about my book… and I have just completed a second season of six programmes talking about opera singers, their stories and funny anecdotes." Ronald Frazer, author of *The Good, the Bad, the Best Forgotten.*

"Margaret Forster loved my book! I have always admired her and, to me, it was the highest accolade." Dulcie Matthews, author of *From Paradise to Eden.*

These are just a couple of comments, but scratch the surface and many authors will say that many positive experiences and other fringe benefits can emerge from self-publishing. From my own experience, I will always recall the pure happiness on the face of my grandfather when he received his self-published book. He died six months later aged 95, and he died happy, knowing that his long and eventful life had been recorded for posterity. Theo Jackson is one man who will not be forgotten.

Self-publishing can be rewarding on many different levels.

WHY WOULD YOU SELF-PUBLISH?

Because sometimes it's the only way

It gives you a chance...

John F X Sundman is an American self-published author who kindly gave me permission to reproduce a summarised version of his views on Why would you self-publish? and Why would you NOT self-publish. He is the author of *Acts of the Apostles* a geeky paranoid technothriller ostensibly about nanomachines and Gulf War Syndrome (in his words).

Emotional rather than logical reasons

You've poured heart and soul into this project, yet the rejection letters pile up. Finally you say "Damn it, I'll publish it myself" – a classic and noble reason to self-publish. You don't care if it makes any money; you just want it out there. Some of our greatest literary geniuses only became known published authors because of their passion, self-belief and self-promotion. This reason in itself justifies the cost – but only if you can afford to write the investment off if your book tanks.

Financial reasons

You achieve far higher royalties, which is a much-claimed benefit. However this argument only stands if you achieve a degree of volume in sales, as what mainstream publishers bring to a lot of authors is broader distribution and marketing. But this isn't always the case, therefore it follows that a self-published title that sells well is worth more to the publishing author than a conventionally published title. If you are both a good writer and a good self-promoter, you stand a good chance. On a personal level, my book received a good reception but if I'd had better distribution and marketing, it would have done a whole lot better.

Political reasons

Trans-national mega-corporations are trying to take over the world and to further their agenda, they need to own and control all media, books, magazines, movies, newspapers, radio, television and the entire internet. Ergo, it is politically bad and immoral to allow one's work to be published with a mega-corporation. One man, Jim Munroe, believes authors have a moral imperative to publish their own works. He is a novelist who left HarperCollins to showcase and propagate indie press alternatives to Rupert Murdoch-style consolidation. (see *www.nomediakings.com*)

Artistic/pragmatic reasons

When you sign a mainstream publisher contract, you surrender content control, design and format control, control over price, the production schedule and marketing & distribution input but most of all, you surrender control over when to give up. Publishers give up really quickly and remainder a book if it doesn't take off in a very small window.

Personally, publishers asked if I was prepared to be completely edited into something more marketable. Whilst I said yes at the time, the offer never came through and now, years later, whilst the money would have been good, I'm glad I don't have a book out on the shelf that I'm not proud of. I'm glad I didn't dumb it down.

Ultimately it depends on why you are publishing. If it's because you want to create something very specific and very particular, your own work of art, then the chances are high that you'll have to self-publish to get it out there.

The Beatrix Potter story

Beatrix Potter self-published with an independent printer after six publishers declined her work. Against the express advice of Frederick Warne, she printed 250 copies of her Peter Rabbit books with black & white illustrations, and sold these at a nominal price to friends and family (Arthur Conan Doyle was one of the proud owners of an original self-produced Peter Rabbit book). They were hugely popular, and, when the concept was re-submitted to Frederick Warne, he agreed to launch the books with coloured pictures, and the rest is history.

Self-publishing is critical when producing a new concept to your own vision

Experiential

This is subjective. It is my unsubstantiated belief that being a writer/publisher is more fun, or at least more unpredictable, than simply being a writer. Writing is a solitary art form, and self-publishing accelerated my emergence from this dangerous cave. Self-promotion forces you to engage with the world in ways that you easily miss out on if somebody else is in charge of marketing and sales. You meet loads of interesting people and create strange strings of connection as you are forwarded from person to person. But this is conjecture since I have never tried any other route!

For posterity

This doesn't need further explanation. In today's world where the written word can be recorded both in print and digitally, each person's story can be preserved forever. Whilst we cannot crack the code of life and immortality, we can immortalise our lives in the written word. Society has a fascination with its past; people invest many hours researching their family tree. Never has it been easier to bring ourselves back to life to our descendents. It's a weird and wonderful thought.

WHY WOULD YOU NOT SELF-PUBLISH?

Financial reasons

It is expensive – a luxury item. You can lose money, not just in direct costs of book production and website creation etc, but also in time and cost invested in book marketing and distribution. These tasks are a full time job in themselves. Ensure you can afford to lose it before you spend it.

There are no guarantees

It is plain and simple – for all your hard work, effort, sweat, commitment and money, there are no guarantees.

It's a lot of hard work

Each part of the process is a full time job in itself and the tasks involved are wide-ranging. Some of them are more challenging and arduous, others are just tedious ie. deliveries and book-keeping… I hate it. I hate it. I hate. I'm not trying to rip anyone off, but life is too short to spend time figuring it all out.

It's a huge learning curve

We have all seen enough house rebuilding programmes to know the complete disasters that can happen when you blindly walk into a territory about which you simply have no experience. And so many people confidently believe that they can waltz into a house rebuilding project and do it with no prior knowledge on a shoe-string budget? Architects, planners, surveyors, builders, electricians, plumbers, bricklayers, decorators, plasterers etc spend years learning their trade.

Whilst the publishing industry is slow to join the 21st century, it cannot be ignored that editors, typesetters, printers, marketers, sales reps, distributors and booksellers actually carry a skill and an expertise that is difficult to learn overnight.

Taking a text from manuscript to publication is a multi-skilled process.

Are you up for it?

Despite how many people advise you against it and bemoan the hard work, the chances are that you'll do it anyway. Hell, when has good, sound advice based on other people's experience ever stopped the committed individual? The mantra clicks into place: *"It's a route. It's the only route. And I'll damn well make it work!"*

All you have to do is...

Become an expert in a wide range of fields very quickly! Don't be put-off; it is all possible. Others have done it before you. The real trick is to understand the publishing process, what you can do and not do yourself, who offers what and what the industry standards are – and for the bits that you really can't do, there are independent suppliers and self-publishing services companies there to do it for you. To help you, this book maps out the publishing process and investigates the wide range of options open to you.

SUMMARY

There are many reasons why you would self-publish, which are not outweighed by the reasons not to self-publish. The advice from 'those who have been there' boils down to three key reasons to:

- Because you can afford to
- Because you have something unique to offer
- Because you have the energy and self-belief for it

These reasons to self-publish are backed up by plenty of advice that other self-publishing authors willingly share, and the over-riding reason not to self-publish is largely for authors who can't afford to, don't have something unique to offer and don't have the energy of self-belief. In other words, the opposite of the reasons why you would.

As John Morrison said, *"only 1% of titles get any real advertising or promotion. If you are prepared to invest time and energy, then your book is already better off than most."*

PART IV

INDEPENDENT SELF-PUBLISHING

The self-publishing author IS the publisher, and many authors forget this. You have, in effect, set up a new business as a publisher, and this chapter analyses each part of the publishing process in the context of what you need to do in order to achieve the high standards expected.

THE PUBLISHING PROCESS

Before ploughing headlong into producing your own book, it is important to acknowledge that, as a self-publishing author, YOU are the publisher. Therefore, it is critical to understand what a publisher actually does. It is WHAT you know that will see you right through the chaos of publishing. The below boxes show an overall flowchart and top-line summary of work, and this section is then followed by an item by item exploration for more detailed knowledge.

Critical assessment
Contract

Edit
- Structural edit ie. pace, characterisation, style, index, appendices, bibliography, illustrations and notes
- copy edit ie. spelling, grammar, punctuation, typos, facts, figures and consistency in presentation
- author answers all arising queries

Create jacket
- Design covers, title and write jacket copy
- Research
- Artwork

ISBNs & registrations
Categorise

Production:
- 1st proof: author & proof-readers; agree formatting ie. fonts, spacing, page layout, headers, footers, binding, size, paper type, other embellishments
- 2nd proof: check revises & last minute questions
- 3rd proof: final check & sign off to production
- brief printer/s: typeset to page proofs
- typeset
- assess proofs

Marketing plan
- create overall sales and marketing plan
- create advanced information sheets (AIS) including author biographies
- promote to trade – distributors / catalogues /sales force presentations
- create sales and promotional materials inc. flyers
- issue review copies; chase up
- plan advertising for trade & press; create artwork

Promote to trade to gain pre-publication sales figures
- Distributors
- Wholesalers
- Co-retailers
- Libraries
- Book clubs (if electing to sell to...)
- Independent booksellers

Publicity:
- Create media list to approach for reviews, interviews, features etc in print, radio & TV
- Write appropriate press release/s, submit & chase
- Organise book tour/events
- Seek ongoing media opportunities
- Festival, talks etc opportunities
- Awards & competitions submissions

Selling other rights:
- Publishing rights abroad* and/or Translation rights*
- Serialisation / extract rights
- Film, TV, radio rights
- Audio rights
- Permissions

**includes representation at book fairs worldwide*

Handle sales:
- Manage customers (stores etc)
- Fulfilment
- Stock control
- Warehousing
- Reprinting
- Sales / Returns
- Invoicing
- Export sales: contracts, printing & shipping

HOW TO PUBLISH YOUR BOOK

Critical assessment

It is impossible to look at your own work objectively – most people cannot proofread their own work. Authors become too familiar with their text and inadvertently skip large tracts of it when copy-reading, and don't even realise they are doing it.

More importantly, does the book say what you intended it to say? Does it tell the story you thought you were telling? Are the characters plausible and consistent? Does the plot unravel in a way to intrigue and interest the reader?

It is very difficult for an author to assess this for themselves, and research shows that most authors receive some form of editing before publication of the book. There are a few very experienced and reliable writers that might slip through the assessment and editing process with admirable speed; everyone else gets thoroughly vetted and corrected.

As a self-publishing author, you would be wise to have a critical assessment done of your work prior to splashing out the cash on submissions to agents, publishers or self-publishing. Invest early to save later.

Self-publishing authors should seek a report on their book's marketability and potential whilst getting the 'literary merit' of the text critiqued. In my role as Marketing Director, I like to get involved at the very outset of a book's publication as my input may alter the emphasis of the book's content and this is discussed in depth in *"What do I have to do to sell a book!"*

Contract

Obviously as a self-publishing author, you don't need a contract with yourself. But it is interesting to see what is covered in a standard contract even if it is just to boost you every now and again when you remind yourself why you're working so hard to produce and sell your book – it is because you are keeping all of those proceeds that many sign away.

Marketing Plan

Prior to publishing a book, you should have a good idea of its key selling points, taking into account the critical assessment you commissioned at the outset. This is a whole process in itself, and as a result, a whole book has been dedicated to this activity as a partner to this book – *"What do I have to do to sell a book!"*

Most of the magazines, websites and societies offer a list of information, guidelines, tips and words of advice and these are all accurate and helpful. But having worked with so many authors who have read all of the advice, many are left wanting to know how to put it into practice.

Edit

The Critical Assessment will provide comments, advice and recommendations for a structural edit ie. pace, characterisation, style, index, appendices, bibliography, illustrations and notes. Whereas an editor will play a large part in this if you have a mainstream contract, the self-publishing author will have to address all of these points himself. On occasion, it may require a fair degree of work and authors tend to work in the dark in this respect. Does it work? Does it not work? There's only one way to find out… send it back to the Editor.

But is the editor right? There are plenty of examples where Editors have criticised work that goes on, in an untouched form, to become much appreciated. Only you, as the creator of the text, can decide what you write, what you change, what you cut and what you ultimately publish.

Once it comes back from the Editor the second time around, he/she should also have thoroughly vetted it for copy checking. All spelling, grammar, punctuation, typos, facts, figures and consistency in presentation should be notified, marked/corrected and you may find yourself answering any last minute queries. The author that seeks perfection will then send it to an independent proofer to proof-read.

A good cover round a poor story merely delays the moment the reader feels disappointed or let-down

The criticism of most self-published works is that they are poorly edited with the occasional typographic error, misplaced punctuation, inconsistent style and spelling mistakes not picked up by MS Word Spell-Checker. This will stand you in very poor stead when you submit your book to a reviewer who receives 100 books a week. The first typo they spot and the book goes onto the Reject pile. You've just wasted all your efforts.

When you send your book out, it must be perfect and you must be proud. If you can't stand behind it 100%, you can be sure that no-one else will.

Sign off only the best -
If you don't stand 100% behind your book,
no-one else will

Sourcing your printer

Much as this seems a very early point to do this, you want to be sourcing your printer now as his input will affect all the cover and page design from here on in. You may as well be working to a specification that he can work from, and his print capabilities will impact on the jacket design. Why spend time creating something that your printer cannot do? Why restrict yourself when the possibilities are huge, and maybe not as expensive as you would think?

Collate printer quotes from a number of areas and not necessarily just in the UK. Printers in Southern Europe are very competitive price-wise and are familiar with UK printing needs, but check language barriers, payment terms and how you'll pay (including current exchange rates) and shipping costs. Delivery times tend to be an influencing factor and you may prefer, in the short term, to use a UK printer for the convenience and lack of language barriers. You will need to check:

- How they need the files ie. PDF is better than MS Word, unless they are typesetting it on your behalf. Bear in mind that transferring a Word document from computer to computer can result in page layout and font changes. If you supply a file in PDF format, nothing changes.
- Review all the paper stock options. Bookshops are very anti the heavier stock papers. Whilst it is the temptation for the self-publishing author to be impressed by the better quality of the paper, the fact is this works against you – not too heavy, not too quality and not too white! Remember, fit to category. Do what the others are doing, unless you are producing a "new concept" book.
- Whilst down-grading the paper quality, ensure you don't get show-through from page to page.
- The paper stock should not be too bright or white; again, take a sample of category standard and get them to match.
- What other embellishments can they offer? ie gloss or matt laminate, selective varnishing, embossing, metallic blocks.
- Do they supply proofs as flats or bound? How many changes can you make and will it cost you?
- Find out reprinting times and costs just in case you get that surprise big order from a large chain store.

Source the printer early
to exploit all the opportunities

Creating the Jacket

The cover of a book makes up 74% of the customer's purchase decision. This fact alone confirms how critical it is to spend time on getting this right. Seek expert advice and don't settle for anything less than perfection.

Choosing a title

This is one area where the 'self-published' element of a book stands out quite starkly, and many self-published titles are badly titled. They are invariably very emotive but relatively meaningless, whereas mainstream published books are usually very well titled. But what makes a good title?

A good title could be any of the following:

- it may intrigue, raise questions, make you wonder ie. *Jonathan Strange and Mr Norrell* by Susanna Clarke. I haven't read the book yet but I am intrigued and will certainly pick it up to consider it
- it may be bizarre, but explained somewhere in the book ie. *Love in a time of Cholera* by Gabriel Garcia Marquez. I was puzzled by the title and loved that one casual moment in the book when the mother observes that her son's symptoms were "like love in the time of cholera."
- it may be emotive and poetic but not holding much meaning. A few that spring to mind (curiously enough all titles with some form of plant involved) are – *The Camomile Lawn, The Judas Tree, Steel Magnolias*. The titles give nothing away, but the link is obvious when you read the book
- it may be self-explanatory ie. *"What do I have to do to get a book published!"* Enough said!

Research the title widely with people - bookshops, total strangers (if you can without alarming them!) and your most outspoken friends and work colleagues. Don't ask them if they like it; just ask them what message it tells them. What would they think the book was about? They are more likely to be more honest, when asked, than a direct 'do you like it?'

Naming a book is like naming a baby. You have to live with it. Have a couple of variations, and repeat them frequently. Talk to other people, naming the book and watching reactions. You might think that "Marion" is a great and unusual name for a little boy, but if everyone winces as you say it, you know you're on the wrong track. The child will suffer the name for a lifetime; your book will simply die a quick death.

Sub-titles or supporting text

The critical task for the cover is to communicate to the potential reader what the book is about and to let them know that it is 'for them'.

Most fiction titles do not have an explanatory sub-title on the front cover as they seek to work on a more emotive level. However, if you think it would help, you could always put a descriptive line as though it is a quote or review.

Barbara Trapido's book *Frankie & Stankie* uses the descriptive line "This is a gorgeous book about growing up... laden with treats, hugely atmospheric..." which tells you the genre of the book when you have a poetic or emotive title.

One self-publishing consultancy, Amolibros, used a line taken from the first paragraph of a book to market it. *The Magic Mooncat* by Lois Fenn has the words 'September 1941 and Hull was on fire' on the front cover, which is immediately evocative.

Jacket design

The most important job the cover can do is to arrest the reader. The jacket is so important that you should get a professional to do it. The jacket design needs to work with the title, supporting front and back cover text as well as being visually arresting. Map out what your cover needs to say about your book then fiddle around with the emphasis of different pieces of communication. What's paramount? What is supportive? Look at several alternatives. If you are briefing a designer:

- have high resolution images of any specific photographs you want to have included
- take along other books or images that define the creative thoughts running through your brain*
- show colours and fonts that you associate with your book
- advise the tone of the book
- make sure they know what it is really about
- and who it is aimed at
- what emotion do you want to inspire in a reader?

A word of advice here… don't be surprised if alternative titling suggestions emerge from the creative process. As the imagery of the cover emerges, sometimes the emphasis of what the title and sub-title is saying needs to be reviewed. The important fact is whether the cover explicitly conveys what the book is about:

- emotion: ie how the book should make you feel ie. uplifted, thoughtful, shocked
- audience: ie. what target does this book aim at – younger/older, male/female
- genre ie. self-help as distinct from business as distinct from education… each category has its own code

Two-thirds of the decision to buy is based on the cover.
Take the time to get it right.

Jacket text

To ensure the central points or key theme of the book are included within the back text, just write out ten random lines about the book, then pick out the most motivating and relevant three statements. People can't take in too much information. They want to know what characters feature; will they identify with them; is it a plausible story; does it echo their life or thoughts at all; will it take them on a journey or provide some light entertainment.

Another good tip is to have an arresting back headline – this might be a review or endorsement, or it might just be a "call to action" that prompts the potential buyer to commit to the purchase ie. Bill Bryson's book *Notes from a Small Island* is head-lined on the back jacket with the words "Laugh out loud funny". This sort of support line certainly caught my attention.

Use the cover to maximum opportunity to catch your audience

Research the cover

As the author, you are very close to the work and will understand what you think you are communicating on the jacket better than someone coming to it afresh. The consummate professional author will do the following:

- Obtain a quality print out of the design, printed to size, in full colour with as close a match to finish as possible on an inkjet printer ie. gloss or pearl finish.
- Go to an artshop and buy 5mm foamboard (they will know exactly what you are asking for even if you don't).
- Cut as many pieces as you need to the overall bookjacket size, and stack them until you have the approximate thickness ie. 5mm, 10mm, 15mm etc. You don't have to be perfect.

- Take this mock-up down to the bookshop/s in your area and ask them what they think. What category would they automatically display it in? What audience do they think it would appeal to? What do they think the book is about? Does it work for them? Do they see it as a potential seller?

Booksellers have always been remarkably helpful and knowledgeable, sharing tips and giving advice completely for free. They often add value in ways that you didn't anticipate; remember, these are the guys who are handling books day in and day out, and they see shoppers browsing for books, see what is being bought and what isn't. They intuitively understand, probably more than they realise, why some books sell and others don't.

Whilst you may also ask friends and family for their views, however honest they want to be they invariably hold just a little bit back, or back off when you start trying to explain why you did this, that or the other.

If the cover doesn't work without explanation, then it doesn't work.

Sometimes designers are resistant to change, but the important element here is not their opinion or your opinion, but the opinion of the market. Listen to the designer's reasons for any reluctance on their part, as they may have a good technical reason for resisting changes ie. stand-out or impact may be compromised, colour codes may be wrong for the category, reproduction quality may be affected. Take on board what they are saying and discuss with them what other ideas or thoughts they might have that take into account the comments from your research, and their expertise as a designer. After all, you both want what is best for the book, as a designer's reputation rests on the success of the cover. They also want your book to be a bestseller.

If the change has been quite fundamental, you might want to go back and check with the bookseller/s. Once you are happy, the cover can then be artworked and made print ready.

Author & designer both want what is best for the book

Think of how the jacket has to perform

Book covers don't just live in a hard-copy, instore book display environment anymore. Whilst it is important to consider how a book cover performs in hard-copy format, many books today are marketed at thumbnail size. Increasingly, books are bought online or from catalogues. Booksellers often choose from catalogues.

Shrink the image down to 2cmx3cm and see how well it works. If there is nothing distinctive about the cover, then make some changes. Ensure that the colour, the copy or the image stands out at thumbnail and in black & white.

Another good acid test to judge standout is to go to Amazon, find all the competitive titles and do "Save as...". Then open up Word or Powerpoint, insert the images and create a page of thumbnails with your book cover placed somewhere in around the middle (but not in the middle!) See how well your book jumps off the page. If it doesn't, then you obviously need to rework it.

Test for standout at thumbnail size amongst competitive titles

Inside front pages

Any book you open has a range of additional pages – a copyright page is obviously a given, but others are optional ie.

a dedication, author biography, index of chapters, a foreword, acknowledgements. But where do these go – at the end or the beginning? Do you need them all? After all, every additional page costs more money.

Your local bookshop is great for research

Study the books in your genre and find out what the standard 'prelim' pages are like. Make a note of what are the standard copyright claims on the copyrights page ie. the ISBN number, date of publication, the publisher contact details, maybe the printer, the jacket designer. Does the chapter index give people enough of an insight as to what is contained within? Sometimes people use indexes as a 'synopsis' to decide whether the book gives them the information (factual books) or excitement (fictional books) they are looking for.

Indexing is a role within itself, and you can buy the skills of a professional indexer, if your book relies heavily on this. This is usually more critical for academic or information-based books.

Author Copyrights and Moral Rights

Firstly, you need to assert your own copyright of the material, and assert your Moral Rights. There are rights that are designed to protect the artistic integrity and reputation of the author.

- They can only be claimed by people, not companies, institutions or employees.
- They must be asserted in writing to the publisher and, once asserted, the publisher must ensure that every copy of the work published and licensed bears the author's name.

There are 4 rights:

- To be identified as the author
- To not have the work treated in a derogatory way
- To not have someone else's work attributed to you
- To have privacy in private photos

Disclaimers

If you have written a book based on fact, you may need to state whether the characters are entirely fictional:

"The characters in this book are fictitious and any resemblance to actual persons, living or dead is purely coincidental."

Maybe you are expressing other people's opinions in your book; therefore you may wish to advise that these are not all your own opinions:

"The opinions expressed within this text are the opinions of the person credited, and do not necessarily reflect the opinions of the author/publisher."

Understanding your copyright

Copyright lasts for 70 years after the end of the calendar year in which the author dies. There is no official register for copyright; and no fees to pay or forms to fill in. You own the copyright of your work as soon as it is written (unless otherwise contracted ie. in employment or working under a specific agreement), although you do not own the copyright over ideas or titles. Therefore, you want to get ideas written down.

You do not need to register the words as copyrighted, although it is always advisable to add the © symbol beside your name and on each page of your manuscript.

BUT having said this, the complexity lies in PROVING who wrote it first. A cheap and easy way to safeguard the proof of when material was written is to print out a hard copy of the text and send it back to yourself. Keep this filed, unopened and the postmark will be adequate proof in a court of law.

Similarly, there is no copyright over titles, although you could be accused of "passing off", if you used a well-known title for your own work.

If you are worried about protecting your idea from being copied when you send your work to agents or publishers, *The Writer's Handbook* suggests that you ask anyone who sees your work to sign a letter confirming that they will not use those ideas or disclose them to anyone else - although, in practice, it can be difficult to get them to sign such a letter. Remember, too, that publishers and agents receive so much unsolicited material that they may already be considering work that is similar to your own.

Further information on copyright:
British Copyright Council: *www.britishcopyright.org*
British Library Copyright Office:
www.bl.uk/services/information/copyright.html

Clearing other people's copyright

This is a nightmare area, if you have used excerpts from other people's text. As the author AND publisher, you need to ensure you have the right to reproduce this, and this can be a tiresome business. You have to track down the existing copyright holder which is no mean feat, then request permission by defining exactly how you wish to use it, in what publication, for what territories and in what context. You might have to pay for this, which on an international level is tedious, involving foreign currency transactions.

Permissions can also prove to be expensive as I found out when researching this book. One national newspaper wanted to charge me £100 for the use of 10 words which is an obscene rate; I suggested I quoted them indirectly but I was informed they would have to charge me £85 per hour to assess legally if I could quote them indirectly!! Fortunately most charges were fairly reasonable.

But this is a legal pre-requisite and if you forget to credit someone as agreed when clearing usage, you will be in breach of the agreement. This can have legal implications if the copyright holder feels strongly about it.

Inside end pages

Fictional titles often have no additional end-pages, although this is a good opportunity to promote the author's other titles, or next book in the series. The end-pages in non-fiction titles can run to many ie. reference list, index, glossary of terms, acknowledgements, appendices. New authors should study these closely to understand how they are structured and laid-out, as there is always the risk of chaos and confusion at this point.

Typesetting

Your book has been edited and the jacket designed. You know what your printer needs and when he needs it by. Now you are ready to move to typesetting the text for a final proof-read, then sign-off.

The criticism that 'self published books often look self-published' also extends to the page layout, substrates and overall production values. These are critical and the self-publishing author would be wise to spend several hours in his nearest bookstore (again!!) analysing published titles in his category. Ensure you can answer the following questions:

- What fonts do they use? At what size?
- What line spacing and margins?
- How have headers and footers been used?
- What sort of titles and in what size/style?
- What does the copyrights page say?
- What prelims and end-pages do they have?
- Does it include an author biography?

- Is the overall 'house style' consistent?
- What is the overall impression of space?

Ensure your book fits to category

Just before you send the final typeset file off to the printer, double-check the following to ensure you have a general quality and tidiness of presentation:

- Is there widowing? Are any words left hanging on their own ie. when they hang over to the next page?
- Are there any rivers ie. gaps that run down a page like a river in a geography book?
- Are the line-ends quite even when not fully justified? Does it look like a spiky mountain range, or a chaotic graph?

Overall production values must look professional

The self-published title MUST 'fit to category' and look every inch as well-produced as the next book along, adhering to all the standard codes. Even if the reader doesn't pick up on the subtleties, your critics will and the buyers will. Don't give them any margin for rejecting your book. Every book that a buyer or a reviewer picks up, he is looking for a reason to not reject the book. Rejection is the first inclination, therefore a book's redeeming features have to hit a buyer/reviewer in the face very quickly.

Follow industry standard procedures

Categorising your book

Imagine you have written a factual book about a famous family ie. the Tudors. Imagine that you incorrectly categorise it, or you use an unfamiliar term that doesn't appear on standard bookseller lists ie. historic drama, because to your mind that is what best captures the essence of your story.

Then you go onto Amazon and find it listed alongside the dramatic plays of Harold Pinter or Shakespeare, or amongst fictional sagas of Daphne du Maurier, or amongst social history educational / academic studies - and nowhere to be seen in amongst the historic, fact-based biographic works of similar texts. Online, you just won't get found via a search facility – and if no-one knows your book exists then you cannot guide people to it.

The same can be said for people browsing the shelves in shops. If your book has been displayed on the wrong shelf in the wrong section, then no-one will find it – even if you go in and ask for it by name. Their computer will show that they may even have stock, but they will point you to the shelf where it SHOULD be once you've described it but someone else has put it in a completely different area of the store.

Remember – bad information in, bad information out. Nobody will find you, and all your work amounts to naught. Have a look on Amazon at similar texts and see where they are listed. Go into your bookshop and see what section they are displayed in. Some publishers are even marking the category on the top right corner of the back cover in order to help bookshops display it correctly. Nielsen have an online table of category codes and you should make the effort to code your work correctly.

Good information in ensures people can find your book

Registering for ISBN numbers

Before you send your book off for first proof, you will need to have registered with Nielsen as a publisher so you can obtain your ISBN (International Standard Book Number) and barcode. In order to do this, you need to have set your price... and in order to do this you need to have done the maths and understood the trade discounts / percentages. Jump ahead to "Setting the Book Price" section (page 160), then return here to resume the process.

To obtain your ISBN number, you need to contact Nielsen Bookdata (0870 777 8710) and request to be registered as a publisher. They will post you a pack which you fill out and return, clearly naming yourself as publisher and stating to where book orders should be routed ie. yourself, your distributor (ie. Gardners, Bertrams, THE, Gazelle etc).

ISBNs can only be bought in batches of ten. These cost £77.50 (currently), and they are registered specifically to one publisher. Once you have returned this, you can then register your book title against one of the ten numbers issued to you.

Currently, ISBN numbers are 10 figure numbers, but as of January 2007 they will be 13 figures - because we are publishing so much that we are running out of 10 figure configurations. It is recommended that publishers doing longer print runs start using both the 10 and 13 figure ISBN numbers.

You can fill the Nielsen bookdata form out online, and the pack contains all this information. Equally you can hand-write and post - but bear in mind that bad information in... If someone mis-reads your hand-writing, you or your book won't be found on computer searches.

Registering the title with Nielsen BookData

Once you have registered yourself as a publisher with Nielsen, which is a one-off process, you then need to register each title or edition that you publish with Nielsen BookData. Every title produced has a unique number, and you will need to complete the Nielsen BookData form for every new title or edition. BookData listings are free, which includes a jacket image but no description. You can, for an additional £100, get an enriched record with much greater information.

Register your book with Nielsen at least 2 months before publication, ideally 4-6 months

Most people believe that delivery of the final printed book should be instantly followed up by the launch and general release. This is not the case. Once you have received the printed copies, you would be advised to use these as 'Review Copies' ie. copies that you will spend the next 3-6 months issuing to book reviewers and endorsers, and this is dealt with thoroughly in *"What do I have to do to sell a book!"* that follows this book.

For the moment you need to ensure you register your book correctly, which means detailing the following information:

- ISBN number
- Price
- Book dimensions (length x width x spine depth)
- Page count and number of illustrations/maps/ photographs
- Description (summary)
- Longer description (optional)
- Category (using Nielsen coding system BIC Basic)*
- Jacket cover

BIC Basic is the standard for defining the core set of information required for book database information. It can appear extremely confusing to the self-publisher as much of it pertains specifically to large publishers. As long as self-publishers fill out the Nielsen BookData pdf correctly, they can rest assured that they have provide good, adequate and relevant information to the book trade.

The importance of good information cannot be underestimated. Nielsen BookData advise that "titles are only added if the information is of sufficiently high quality."

BookData now has "unique facilities" in place to test and verify that information, including using Nielsen BookScan sales information for verifying publication dates and prices notified by publishers and distributors.

You may also see a reference to ONIX. This is a standard XML format for delivering product information to booksellers – again, not really relevant for self-publishers.

Further information can be found on Nielsenís website
www.nielsenbookdata.co.uk
FYI - you can download the Nielsen bookdata pdf from
www.indepublishing.com

Registering with Bowker Books in Print

Several years ago, there were two book data companies – Whitakers and Nielsen. It was complex, confusing and time-consuming, so the two companies merged. It became a lot easier for everyone.

Now, just to re-complicate the process, the American book data-collating company, Bowker, have recently entered the UK market! To be thorough, you will want to upload your book information to Bowker as well (*www.bowkerlink.com*) and it is a far more fiddly system than Nielsen.

Registering with PubEasy®: *www.pubeasy.com*

PubEasy®, the Global Publishing e-Marketplace, represents the new standard in e-commerce for the global bookselling industry. Thousands of booksellers from over 110 countries spanning North America, Europe and Asia are using PubEasy to facilitate access to order placement, order tracking, price, title and availability data over the Internet with participating publishers, distributors and wholesalers, more quickly and cost-effectively. Booksellers with a PubEasy password can directly access any participating Affiliate web site on the PubEasy network. PubEasy web sites provide:

- Up-to-the-minute information on title, price, and stock availability
- Order placement and confirmation even when customer service departments are closed
- Order status inquiry capabilities, for all orders and back orders
- High-volume inquiries and ordering with /TRANSACT, including POS system compatibility
- Searchable e-Catalogs of title information
- Single password login to a network of participating publisher, distributor and wholesaler Affiliate web sites
- Fast-loading, clean, easy-to-use screens across all sites
- Simple registration process

Adding a Barcode

The barcode contains your unique ISBN number which enables shops to swipe the book through their systems and complete the sale. Without a barcode and ISBN number, book shops may be reluctant to sell your book as they have to key the price in manually. Booksale rankings are also calculated against this ISBN via the number of sales through the tills. Private sales and non-ISBN numbered books do not contribute to booksale rankings.

You can buy a barcode software which will generate barcodes for you. Equally, some printers will sort out the barcode for you, and some will even provide you with an ISBN if you don't want to buy a batch of 10. But, bear in mind, the ISBN number is then registered to them as the printer, rather than you as the publisher. The implications being that any enquiries or orders for your book will be directed straight through to the printer who is registered as the publisher of your book. This might be by conscious agreement between yourself and your publisher as they may be managing fulfilment on your behalf. If they are not doing this, then shops will have a tricky time trying to locate your book.

What is Legal Deposit?

In the UK, it is a legal pre-requisite in the UK to lodge books with the following bodies and booksellers within one month of publication:

1. The British Library
2. Bodleian Library, Oxford
3. Cambridge University Library
4. The National Library of Scotland
5. The National Library of Wales
6. Library of Trinity College, Dublin

Publishers do not have to complete any form or register with the Agency for the Legal Deposit Libraries. Merely submit material to the Agency below together with a delivery note indicating publisher address details to which the Agent can send an acknowledgement of receipt:

The British Library, Legal Deposit Office
Boston Spa, Wetherby, West Yorkshire LS23 7BY
Tel: +44 (0)1937 546268 (monographs) / 546267 (serials)

For the other libraries, send books to:
Agency for the Legal Deposit Libraries
100 Euston Street, London NW1 2HQ
Phone: 020 7388 5061

If you are interested in the deposit of pure electronic content either by e-mail to *LDO-Electronic@bl.uk* or by FTP, please contact Andrew Davis on telephone: 01937 546535 or email: *andrew.davis@bl.uk*. The Agency is currently reviewing its processes for acquiring works in electronic format. If you are interested in the deposit of electronic content by email please contact them.

Other important databases

There are other online lists where you should register your book– Amazon.co.uk being an obvious one. Others you may consider are Googleprint.com and Abebooks.com.

How to use Amazon

Amazon advise publishers to add as much information as possible to give their title maximum opportunity.

Amazon have several different methods of selling books and the information is all on their website, but to help you…

To simply add a title to Amazon, go to the Catalogue Guide on their website. This will tell you to email the details to *book-catalogue-dept@amazon.co.uk* and request complete details for new title submission. It also directs you on how to upload book jackets, and more in depth information such as book description, publisher and author comments, author biography, table of contents and back jacket text. The more information the better, so it is wise to put as much descriptive and author biography information as possible.

If you subsequently need to alter your submission, email *book-typos@amazon.co.uk*. This takes a couple of days, and you must remember to email with ISBN number, your name and contact details.

What is Amazon Advantage?

This is, in effect, an enhanced service for publishers to sell via Amazon. All books have a 24 hour availability listing with no upper or lower limit on items stocked. They offer quick payment terms and a Sales/Inventory report is available online at any time. Amazon monitor the inventory and automatically email requests for new stock.

The cost for this is a £23.50 annual charge including VAT and slightly higher per unit percentages, with books taking a 60% discount ie. the publisher gets 40% of selling price.

As a member of Amazon Advantage you can also buy a range of promotional services which include the "Look inside" text-search system and advertising or promoting your book on the site. The "pairing" system is done automatically by the computer system.

What is Amazon Marketplace?

This allows sellers to sell books (new or used) on the same page as the brand new version of the book. As a seller, you can sell the book for less.

Listing your items takes little more than a minute, and you get a postage credit to help with the cost of p&p. You are charged a 75 pence closing fee and 15% of the price of the item, and the profits from your sale are deposited directly into your bank account.

Remember that Amazon.co.uk and Amazon.com are two separate databases. To get onto Amazon.com you need US distribution with a major distributor; this means that you either need to have a comprehensive and evidential marketing plan that demonstrates how you are driving sales and demand – or you have to pair up with a POD publisher who will put you on US databases for a very reasonable sum.

What is Googleprint.com?

Google have created a program which allows publishers to promote books on Google for free, much like the Amazon Search Inside system. Whether a large publisher or a small press, the Google Print program enables you to add your books to Google's search results and:

- Increase your book's visibility at no cost
- Attract new readers and boost book sales
- Drive qualified traffic to your website
- Earn new revenue from Google contextual ads

Either upload a pdf file or post the book to Googleprint, and they will add it to their index.

There has been much debate over this system, as authors do not receive any income from the 20% that the searching public can download; yet advocators of the facility argue that it increases the volume and range of books sold as it enables people to find the books they are searching for.

What is Abebooks.com?

Abebook's literature claims that it is the world's largest online marketplace for books with over 12,000 booksellers from around the world selling over 20,000 books a day. Abebooks was historically a market place for booksellers specialising in out-of-print, hard-to-find and/or collectable books, but has now opened up its offer to all books and booksellers. There are low start-up costs for booksellers to join the marketplace with low rates of commission, flexible shipping rates, easy inventory management systems and simple account management.

Printer proofs

You will have agreed already in what form the proofs will come back to you ie. either as loose leaves, with the cover as a flat or glued (which is even better). Given the choice, ask for a bound proof and assess it for:

- errors – see Last Chance Proofing below.
- covers should lie flat. Acid test is to leave them on a side table in the fall of a table-light for a short while, or in a warmish room for 24 hours.
- check the laminate all the way round. It should not be flaking or peeling on any edge.
- check the bend of the book ie. hold the closed book in one hand and bend it along the length. It should give and bend easily. If it feels rigid, then the book buyer will dismiss it. Paperback readers prefer a lighter weight book they can carry around, and buyers will dismiss a book printed on too good a paper stock.
- break the spine and drop the book on the floor; no pages should fall out. If they do, then the glue job is poor and it won't stand up to the rigours of holiday or bath-time reading.
- margins – check that the gutter is wider than the edge margins so readers don't have to break the spine just to read the words in the centrefold
- are you happy with the top and bottom margins, and position of page number

Last chance proofing

It is a curious fact of life that the text looks and reads very differently once it is presented as a book. Therefore take the time out to sit down and read the book as a newcomer to the text might. Suddenly there are flaws, glaring mistakes and inadequate descriptions all over the place, but it is best to catch them now. Sit yourself down with a red pen, and use it. Don't feel bad about changes – after all, the chances are that you are paying for them anyway and it's just a shame you didn't pick them up earlier. Just remember that just because you might be prepared to ignore or overlook them, it doesn't mean the book reviewer, buyer or reader will.

What you choose to sign off reflects on you and you alone

Assessing the final product

Check that all your changes have been implemented, and re-test one copy of the book for all the quality measures as mentioned above. Report any faults or issues immediately; and get it rectified before final payment. Problems do arise, as Preethi Nair found out when her book came back with a page missing. She noticed this immediately, and the missing page was duly printed and sent to her, but timing was a real problem as she was launching the book the next day. Preethi spent the night Pritt-sticking the missing page into each book.

Give yourself enough time to correct errors

Setting up trade accounts

There are 4,500 bookshop outlets, which are a mix of book chainstores, independent booksellers, specialist bookshops, co-retailers and bargain bookshops. They all hold accounts with the main distributors and wholesalers who hold stocks of the book on behalf of the publisher; mainstream publishers tend to hold accounts with distributors as well as direct to booksellers.

Small or self-publishers will need to set up an account with a distributor and this will enable access to selling to both the chains and independent booksellers. Distributors will take 40-55% which includes the bookseller percentage.

When choosing a wholesaler and/or distributor, you must consider that you (as a small fish in a very big sea) may get lost within a large organisation (ie. Gardners, Bertrams, THE).

Meet with them and check to see how their systems work ie. does it meet the needs of a small or self-publisher? Can you log on to monitor sales yourself? You may choose to go with a smaller company (ie. Central, Gazelle) if they prove they can provide a more personalised service.

If you have chosen to use Amazon Marketplace or Abebooks.com, remember that you are technically the bookseller and therefore this requires ongoing management. Amazon will take around 60% of each booksale, which obviously does not include the post & packing, as you are fulfilling it direct.

Wholesalers

Wholesalers deal with the book trade. They will purchase a stock of your book, making it available to their own booktrade accounts. They usually offer terms around 35-45% of the actual sale price of book, which includes the bookseller discount. Therefore, if your book retails at £6.99 you will receive £3.84 per book back from them. If they put it into a promotion and discount it, you will receive 45% of the discounted price.

Wholesalers do not do any active marketing on specific titles, although some will specialise in either

(i) certain genres (ie. educational, medical, secular/religious etc) or
(ii) certain channels (ie selling into Garden Centres, Gift Shops, petrol station forecourts etc.)

In my experience, any wholesaler operating a specific channel will charge a slightly higher percentage because of the value of their database. This negative is weighted against the fact that they tend to order in quantity because they have a ready audience and can reach many outlets.

Distributors

Distributors are slightly different from wholesalers, bundling a whole raft of bookselling tasks under one roof – warehousing stock, billing, fulfilling and selling. Their services include sales representation to bookstores and wholesalers.

This is not an exclusive service (unless your contract states otherwise), and you can have several distributors promoting your titles. One caveat to this is that a bookseller seeking urgent stock of a title may order it from 2-3 distributors, accept the first one in and possibly return the others. You may find your 'returns' rate increases in proportion to the quantity of distributors you use.

Standard terms are 90 days, and it is typical for distributors to hold back some percentage against possible returns. So, if you use several distributors, you may find yourself bank rolling an even bigger stock in the market, which is only worth remaindering as/when it comes back.

Distributors and wholesalers are studied comprehensively in "What do I have to do to sell a book!"

Prepare an Advance Information Sheet (AIS)

The trade will require an Advance Information Sheet (AIS) which provides them with a comprehensive specification of your book. Using the basic information provided to Nielsen (and Bowker etc), create a neatly laid out one-page A4 sheet that you can either print or email. This information should include:

- Book title
- Author/s
- Illustrators/ photographers (if any)
- ISBN number
- Price
- Book dimensions (length x width x spine depth)

- Page count and number of illustrations/maps/ photographs
- Description ie. as 3-4 bullet points
- Target audience
- Genre of book; optionally including the Nielsen category as an extra piece of information
- Front jacket design (if emailing, ensure it is a small file).

(go to *www.indepublishing.com* for a downloadable example).

An AI sheet forms the basis of most communication to the market

OTHER CRITICAL ACTIVITIES FOR SELF-PUBLISHERS

DOING THE MATHS

Bearing in mind the old adage that *"the secret of success is in the preparation"* there is still another step to go through before you leap onto the self-publishing venture... you need to do the maths.

Nobody should proceed with a self-publishing venture if they are a little bit strapped for cash, or are seeing publishing as a route out of financial straits. It's not, and nobody out there should pretend otherwise.

Firstly, teach yourself some basic accounting skills, and ensure you are thorough, so you don't overlook a cost that lands you in the proverbial poo further down the line. Visit an accountant and understand how to lay out monthly calculations, know what's deductible and/or a viable expense. Claim everything you can and nothing you can't. Know at what income-level you have to become VAT registered, or whether it is worth your while becoming VAT registered anyway.

Start collating costs

Using the SAMPLE CALCULATION (page 162), list out all of the costs you have collated in order to produce your book. Make sure you allow generously for items such as fulfilment if you are doing this independently. If, however, you have employed the services of a wholesaler, you can work this out more precisely with their help.

In order to begin to get a picture of your potential profit/loss calculations, you will need to set a book price.

This works on the assumption that all 1,950 books sell – and that is a lot of books to shift, particularly for a book by an unknown novelist. I will have to really work my socks off and do lots of events and self-promotion.

SETTING THE BOOK PRICE

What's the maximum your book can sell for?

A good start-point is to work out what is the maximum price you think you could sell your book for. Go into your local bookshop (they will SO know you by now!) and see what similar and competitive titles in your category or genre are selling for. How well are they selling (ask at the desk) or are sales heavily dictated by discounts? This will inform you whether the price you need to sell at is realistic.

GP Taylor says that the price setting he selected was an early mistake he made on *Shadowmancer*. He set it at £5.99 against a unit cost of £2.25, believing this to be a good mark-up. But once bookseller percentage, fulfilment and invoicing had been added, he says he earned barely anything from each sale. This didn't take into account his personal time investment in fulfilment, endless trips to the post-office, selling-in, marketing, book events etc. *Shadowmancer* is a sizeable book, hence the per unit cost price, and it could easily have withstood another pound on the price point.

Children's books sell well around the £4.99-£6.99 area; whereas Adult fiction can tolerate £6.99-£8.99. Non-fiction can peak around the £9.99 mark, and informational paperbacks can vary between £10-15. These are, of course, all before discounts.

What's the minimum your book must sell at?

After visiting your bookshop and discovering that your fictional crime thriller (paperback, 220 pages, standard format, unknown author) can reasonably expect to sell at £6.99, you then need to work out what is the lowest you can afford to sell the book at. The difference between the lowest and highest is sadly not going to be a huge amount. Whilst in the music industry, reproducing CD's is an incremental cost, in the publishing industry the price per book remains a fairly chunky amount.

Standard mark-up

Some people suggest an 8x mark-up. Even if you just took the print cost alone, this would often fire you out of a credible price range. And if you have done a print-on-demand publication, then forget it. You won't ever be doing an 8x mark-up.

For argument's sake, I have a print quote of £2,000 (+ VAT) for my 220 page paperback, no illustrations, for 1000 copies. That makes them £2.00 per copy. I can reasonably sell them at £6.99 which is a 3.5 times mark-up.

If I get 2,000 books, the increase in cost is incremental - £2,250. Suddenly, I have a £1.13 per book cost, therefore can mark-up by 6x which is a lot healthier in order to cover all the other costs. But I must remember to add on my other operational costs.

Potential profit

Look at the calculation on the next page which lists out all of the costs to get a 220 page paperback book to print. The profit sounds reasonable, and you would be happy to have covered all of the costs to date. Then you have to consider your fee time to create this "product".

SAMPLE CALCULATION

	Outoing	Incoming	
Developmental costs			
Editing	£ 350.00		
Design	£ 300.00		
Proof reading	£ 150.00		
Typesetting	£ 250.00		
Registrations - ISBN	£ 77.50		
	£1,127.50		
Production costs			
Print proof	inc.		
Print x 1000 copies	£2,000.00		
Marketing			
Review copies x 50	£ 100.00		
Postage & packing	£ 50.00		
Phone calls p/quarter	£ 150.00		
Travel p/quarter	£ 100.00		
Sales			
Discounts if 1950 books sell)		£5,452.20	
P&P (if 143 unique deliveries)	£1,000.00		
TOTAL		**£9,979.70**	
Profit calculations			
Divided by 2000 books	£ 4.99	cost per book	
POTENTIAL PROFIT:	**£ 2.00**	**per book**	
OVERALL PROFIT:	**£3,900.00**	**for 1,950 books**	

CAVEATS TO CONSIDER WHEN DOING THE MATHS

Fulfilment is often incremental

Fulfilment can get expensive as books can often go out one by one. This means that effort per sale is not representative of the profit made out of that sale. Different booksellers demand different percentages, and then it is often sale or return that means the book isn't sold until some vague time in the future when a cheque suddenly arrives – or the book does.

Reinvest for the second print run

The other critical factor to remember is reinvestment. Let's pretend you have sold the first 1,950 and have your £3,900 profit. Are you going to reprint? Another 2000 books will cost around £2,250. That will leave you with £1,650 profit, which also has to fund all the fulfilment operational costs.

Do you need to reprint?

Some books have saturated their market by the time they have sold 2000 copies, and before you rush off to get another 2000 printed, you will need to think carefully about how many more potential readers you can reach out to and make aware of your book.

Every title has a saturation point, and for most fictional titles it is impossible to determine what this is. For some books, the market may be saturated having sold only 100 copies. Other books enjoy much higher ceilings, running into the millions.

The best method of remaining responsive to market demand is to calculate print runs that provide adequate profit if they all sell, but won't leave you bankrupt if they don't. Keep a tight rein on stock control and have a good relationship with your printer to ensure they are reactive to any urgent print runs you may require.

The cost of sale/return

Sale/Return is an industry standard. It's tough on the big publishers but can cripple the small independent or sole publisher. Sometimes books are returned in a less-than-new condition and cannot be sold at cover price. If it is damaged, worn or dusty, your book can only be remaindered which won't actually cover the cost of printing - you might get more for pulping the book instead of selling it.

I know of some instances where a major chain has ordered 20,000 books and returned 8,000. That's enough to make the individual go bust, obviously. They were returned in good, sellable condition, but nonetheless… to have 8,000 books that you thought were sold to be unexpectedly returned to you is a painful, and expensive, experience.

Arguably, when a large chain orders in such volume, there should be some form of guarantee for the "little man". Surely over a certain volume, it has to be a firm sale even if at a higher than usual percentage? Book clubs might take a hefty percentage, but at least they buy them firm. The books don't all come tumbling back at you.

Covering fee-time

How much actual **time** have you put into the book - a dedicated six months? A year? Remember, a lot of work goes into the actual creation of this baby:

- writing the book and its many re-drafts
- supervising its production
- learning about publishing
- making the contacts (online & offline)

- setting up the accounts
- marketing the book (events, press releases, databases, follow-ups, interviews etc)
- doing your invoicing and accounts
- hours spent queuing up at the post-office

Surely this came to 10 hours a day, 5 days a week for 6 months…1300 hours at what, £15 per hour is £19,500 for six months work. Sounds about right for what you COULD be earning if you weren't at home writing a book. To recoup that plus all the development and direct costs you would have to sell… 14,200 books! That would just knock you into profitability. Easy peasy lemon squeezy!

Amortise it!

Fee time, as well as the Developmental Costs, can be amortised over time. They don't vary with ongoing print run, but remain fixed. Therefore, you could either front-end load the calculations as we have done on the Sample Cost page, or you could spread it over an optimistic 5 print runs of 2000 each. But it may take several years and dedicated hard-work to sell 10,000 books, if you ever achieve it. And there is a good reason why publishers only support a title for its first year – after that initial launch and marketing impetus, interest dies down.

Earning pay-back from writing

In many instances, the 'pay back' from publishing comes in many different forms. Whilst it would be great if a book provided some actual income, sometimes people get a renewed sense of value just from the recognition or achievement alone. Others have found new careers as a result of their book publishing endeavours.

Income from sale of rights

Throughout the book we have solely looked at income from the sale of the book, and not from the sale of rights. Obviously, most publishers and agents are deriving a considerable amount of income from rights. As independent authors achieve publishing success, they are increasingly earning income from sale of rights but it can be a bewildering territory to enter at the outset.

This is covered further in "What do I have to do to sell a book!"

MANAGING THE SALES

This is, by all accounts, the area where most self-publishing authors struggle the most is tedious and time-consuming activity and is often the reason that self-publishing authors seize a mainstream publishing deal when it is offered to them.

Warehousing / storage

The larger the print run, the more space required to warehouse books, and this obviously costs money. Take this into account when planning your print run. What you might save on volume print, you may spend in warehousing.

The average self-publishing author is likely to be storing only a couple of thousand of one title, but you still need a spare room for this. Nobody ever really pauses to think about how much space 1000 books take up, or how heavy they are. Don't plan to store them upstairs in your house. Firstly, you will exhaust yourself carrying them upstairs and secondly, the floor joists may not be able to take the strain. Honestly!

If you have a garage, then clear a wall and stack the books up against the wall as though laying bricks (purely for reasons of stability). Obviously the garage needs to be well-insulated and dry, but I'm sure that goes without saying. It is advisable to ensure there is an air-gap between the floor and the books ie. by building your own wooden platform just enough to raise it off the ground by a small amount.

If you live in a small flat or upstairs apartment, the temptation is to scatter the boxes around friend's houses, but you will lose track of the stock. You may as well remain in control by paying for some warehouse space – it's not THAT expensive.

Fulfilment

Book orders come in from a variety of sources – Nielsen teleordering, distributors and wholesalers, independents, online sellers, direct from customers. Given the complexity and time-consuming nature of this task, publishers will often outsource it; the biggest publishers have large distribution and fulfilment departments or partners.

Fulfilment is reputedly the soul-destroying part of self-publishing. You think you are an author, but suddenly you are Post-room boy, now on first name terms with all of the counter staff in the local post office, and you can't move in your house for all the brown paper, tape, labels, boxes and bubble-wrap.

Packing area

It is advisable to set yourself up a sturdy table beside the book storage area. Have a good stock of padded envelopes, bubble-wrap, brown paper, boxes, tape, labels, stamps etc. Buy these in bulk from one of the stationery suppliers, and ensure you always pack books well. Review copies can go in padded envelopes and actual sale copies should go in boxes. Pack books well for posting as books that arrive damaged may well get returned to you. It is worth asking your local bookstore if they have any spare, or getting some of the wine boxes from the supermarket.

Invoicing and royalties

"Arghghg! Invoicing! I'm not an accountant. I hate doing the books! I don't understand tax." is the cry up and down the country from self-employed people in any business. Unfortunately, it is an essential part of the process – so you had better get your head round it, set aside a regular time each week and do it little and often. File thoroughly and pay an accountant to do your year end returns. It is money well spent.

Sale or Return

The chains and independents accept books in on a Sale or Return basis. This is an age-old habit as many of the independent booksellers were small stores who couldn't afford to buy in a wide range of stock. To entice bookstore owners to display their titles, publishers offered a sale or return principle. If, for example, the book hadn't sold after one year, the store could return it. In today's world of 140,000 NEW titles per annum across 4,500 bookstores, there is a vast movement of books. This movement only incurs a cost, not a sale or profit, and the standard sale/return period is now 90 days. Barely long enough to get a marketing campaign going.

If reprinting is a thorny issue, then Sale or Return is positively scary. What happens if a major bookseller believes that your book is going to sell REALLY well, and they order 2,000 of them for the Christmas frenzy? You celebrate all over Christmas, then in February all 1,900 books come tumbling back. Maybe they only sold 100.

Stock control and reprinting

With publishers, the stocks are managed and re-order quantities carefully assessed with the full experience of the sales teams and stock control manager. Publishers will always look for the biggest print run against likely projected sales, in order to get the best cost per unit. It takes an experienced and thorough sales force to provide any degree of accuracy on projections, carefully weighted against the cost of returns and any income derived from remaindering or pulping.

For the self-publisher, stock control can be tricky... how many to reprint and when? What are the chances of a big order suddenly coming in? Being fore-armed with knowledge of your printer's lead times is important, just in case you get *that* phone call from Waterstones requesting 5,000 copies of your book!

Over and above this decision, however, is the thorny issue of reinvesting any income to date in order to reprint (see Doing the Maths section on page 159). The self-publishing author will need to determine whether he has reached market saturation after the selling the first print run, or is there still ongoing market demand?

SERVICES YOU MAY REQUIRE
WRITING & EDITORIAL SERVICES

There are a number of writing and editorial services companies available, and below I have listed some that I found on the internet. I have not worked with most of them, but they are listed below because they sounded as though they had a thorough offer and purpose. The company descriptions are the companies' own. But firstly a word on editing:

THE IMPORTANCE OF EDITING

"Editing Matters" by Hilary Johnson

The author whose book is being published by a traditional-style publishing house is lucky in more ways than the obvious. He (this should be taken as reading 'he or she' hereafter) will be working with an editor who may recommend changes which will make the book even better than it already is and there will be a copyeditor to look over the typescript not only for errors of spelling and punctuation but for those of fact and any other points of detail or infelicities of style which may need attention. As a final stage in the polishing of what everyone hopes will be a flawless finished product, the author will be given the task of checking the proofs for any literals or other easily remedied slips which may have escaped notice.

Despite all this, most of us have probably had the experience of reading a published book and finding the odd spelling mistake or some such. It's remarkable how even the smallest error can pull the reader up short and momentarily divert attention from the story or non-fiction text.

At least in these circumstances the author can disclaim responsibility. Factual errors, though, are another matter. The finest of copyeditors, armed with the most extensive of personal reference libraries and with the internet on tap, cannot be expected to know everything about every subject. It is for the author to ensure absolute accuracy with respect to factual detail, quotes, sources and so on.

But what any author can know as a certainty, no matter how abstruse the area of knowledge, there will be some reader somewhere just waiting to discover an inaccuracy and to pen a know-better letter to the publisher. Of course, if a publisher receives too many such letters pointing out too many errors, then confidence in that author will swiftly evaporate.

The position for the self-publisher is different: inasmuch as he has chosen to take an independent route, he is responsible for virtually every aspect of the book's finished appearance. If the pages are poorly punctuated, littered with spelling errors, with dubious grammar and even just a few factual inaccuracies, he will, quite simply, strike anyone who picks up the book as someone who has not learned how to use that most basic tool of the writer's craft, the language itself. It might be that he is a spell-binding storyteller, or a truly riveting expounder of his specialist subject, but these qualities will be overlooked by readers distracted by a plethora of wrongly-placed possessive apostrophes or enraged by some trivial but consistently appearing wrong 'fact'.

(There are a few best-selling authors whose work needs heavy editing in order to deal with their inadequacies in these matters, but whose books are such compelling page-turners and such huge money-spinners that it's worth this extra labour. However, these are largely writers who established both themselves and their loyal readership some time ago; these days, busy editors are all too often put off by a poorly-presented typescript which promises to demand many hours of a copyeditor's time.)

The most literate and perfectionist of self-publishing authors can still fail to spot every single mistake in a typescript. Close familiarity with a text can mean that it is not seen with the freshest of eyes. For this reason, even if the author knows himself to be completely competent in these matters, it makes sense to have somebody reliable go through the typescript before the material goes to the printers.

It is important that this check is done on the page and not on screen, since errors on the computer screen are more likely to be missed. Also, it is easier to indicate corrections on the page.

A friend or family member in whom the author has total confidence may be ideal to carry out this scrutiny. Some of the companies offering self-publishing services include editing either as an option or as a part of the package. (Many work to high standards, but I have seen a few books where, for instance, the same error in the punctuation of dialogue occurs throughout. It behoves the author to be insistent upon seeing proofs and meticulous in reading and correcting them.)

Using the services of a professional copyeditor is one way to ensure that, allowing for the occasional human lapse, something close to perfection is achieved. A well-designed cover, a quality production job and a flawless text should leave the author satisfied that he has done his best to produce a book of which he can feel proud, certainly from the presentation point of view.

Content, though, may be another matter. I have not so far touched upon the kind of editing which deals with writing quality. Usually, I advise our clients that it is sensible to have the typescript professionally appraised before it is copyedited. Almost invariably, such an assessment identifies at least some weaknesses or areas needing attention and it seems pointless to pay the costs involved in copyediting a piece of work which is likely to be substantially rewritten.

Some authors want to proceed with copyediting and self-publishing regardless of the fact that their book, with guidance and a little more effort on their part, could be much improved, with the consequence that there are some pretty indifferent self-published books in existence.

To generalise, but also judging by those authors who use my service, writers of non-fiction books are more likely than aspiring novelists to have produced a typescript which can go straight ahead with copyediting and which requires little or nothing in the way of radical alteration. Naturally, there are some novelists and authors of children's books to whom the same applies, but the pitfalls for the relatively inexperienced writer are potentially greater and more numerous in these areas.

Hilary Johnson

COMPANIES THAT OFFER EDITING SERVICES

The Hilary Johnson Author's Advisory Service

A proven reading and criticism service for a range of writers - novelists, writers of short stories and children's books and authors of full-length non-fiction. We also provide a specialist advice service for science fiction/fantasy, radio/TV/film scripts and poetry.

Further to the above advice on editing and in regard to my service, we can only advise authors on the basis of a combination of long experience and the individual's expressed needs. If it's copyediting which is wanted, whatever the quality of the material, we can provide it. After all, for the author of a not-very-good book, this will at the very least mean the avoidance of embarrassing errors or displays of ignorance. And for the author of the really good book, well, that final polish is no less than his work deserves!

Our objective is to help writers achieve publication. We can't, alas, wave a magic wand for every aspiring author, but we can:

- provide a thorough, practical and frank criticism
- explain what is needed to give a typescript commercial appeal
- show how to submit a professional-looking typescript
- give authors of outstanding talent a direct route to a leading literary agent

Contact details

Web: *www.hilaryjohnson.demon.co.uk*
Email: *enquiries@hilaryjohnson.com*
Phone: 01485 578594

Publishers UK Ltd

Publishers UK Limited aims to help talented writers to get published. We focus on the following areas - crime, romance, mystery, sci-fi, literary and non fiction writers, and have a number of services to support authors including:

- an in depth script surgery service to assist writers in bringing their work to a publishable standard
- a digital publishing service, in which the cost of publishing, marketing and distribution is shared with the writer

At Publishers UK Ltd we are all writers, and we have all, at some stage in our careers, experienced the soul-destroying arrogance and indifference that characterises the publishing industry today - from the pro-forma rejections that tell you that nobody has even bothered to read the book (which you might have spent five or ten years of your life writing), to the patronising submission guidelines that appear on every publishers' website from Los Angeles to London.

In a market where there are too many writers, and where most publishers and agents are happy to take on perhaps one new writer every couple of years, unpublished authors, however talented, face an almost impossible struggle. For even if they manage to get their work read, and even if the publisher in question considers the book to be superb, if it doesn't fit with that publisher's marketing lists, it will not be published.

It is a sad and shameful fact that the vast majority of publishers have abdicated their responsibility to the art of literature, and their sole aim is to market and sell books. The potential of these books is decided, not by publishers with a love of literature, but by money men, on the basis of market research and statistics. If Graham Greene had been born today, and had to compete with Victoria Beckham's Memoirs in trying to get *The Human Factor* published, he wouldn't stand a chance.

Let's face it, it is a cliché, but no less true for that, if the great authors who made the 20th century the golden age of the novel attempted to get published today, most of the greatest novelists of our age would have been lost without trace. What is depressing is that right now great novels and great novelists *are* vanishing without a trace, because our publishers have become factories and our agents have become commodity brokers.

Contact details

Web: *www.publishersukltd.co.uk*
Email: *editor@publishersukltd.co.uk*
Phone: 01243 576016

Writing Ltd

Writing Ltd Literary Consultancy was founded by people working as literary agents or editors to provide writers with a place to come for advice and informed editorial feedback on their writing.

As part of our editorial services you will receive an honest and thorough report on your work, providing you with constructive criticism and specific examples to work from to enhance strengths and work on weaknesses in your writing. You can determine what kind of an input you would like by choosing from one of our services (see website).

Writing Ltd has strong links within the agenting and publishing industry and if we find anything that has great potential we will contact you about this with a view to sending it on to an agent and discuss the next step.

If you choose to go ahead with our manuscript assessment and appraisal service you will receive back a copy of your manuscript with any specific annotations and a report of approx 7-12 pages in length, covering all the critical areas and this is itemised on the website.

A good plot and strong characters combined with your writing skills are the essence of a good novel. Your plot and characterisation are as important as your writing whether you are ready to submit to an agent or whether you want to ensure your writing flows around a solid structure.

When you are working as closely as you are to your plot and your characters it is easy to overlook weaknesses and holes. A trained eye can help to bring attention to these points and suggest ways to improve or strengthen these areas.

Contact details
Web: *www.writing.co.uk*
Email: *info@writing.co.uk*
Phone: 01799 544659

The Writer's Workshop

A manuscript assessment and editorial service available for writers who need help with a manuscript.

If your manuscript reaches the required standard, we will use our excellent contacts with leading London agents to ensure that your book is read with close attention. We understand that publication is your ultimate aim and we will do what we can to help you achieve this goal.

Today's publishing industry is competitive, crowded and commercially-oriented. That means it can be hard for new authors to get a look in. Our principal aim is always to do all we can to help our clients bring their work to the level required by today's market. But it is not always possible to achieve publication by a conventional route. In such cases, we will always be honest about your chances and are happy to give you guidance in the realm of responsible self-publication. We never charge for introductions to agents or publishers. You are never obliged to accept our recommendations, nor to go with the agents or publishers that we may recommend.

A range of services including a reading by a qualified editor and provision of a full report – circa 3,000 words long; tailored to your specific needs. We discuss this with you and stay in touch, acting as your guide in the publishing market.

We have a second read option where the consultant will read your revised manuscript, and send you a summary of issues still needing work. We also offer 'budget' (short read) option as well as mentoring if you want a long-term working relationship with a skilled editor.

Contact details
Web: *www.writersworkshop.co.uk*
Email: *enquiries@writersworkshop.co.uk*
Phone: 01865 820943

THE TOP TEN WRITING PROBLEMS

By Hilary Johnson

- Weak and ill thought-out plot, often of insufficient strength or complexity to sustain a novel of any substance.
- Lack of pace/narrative drive. A tendency to dwell upon unimportant detail and irrelevancies.
- Failures of ordinary logic, both in characterisation and the development of a story. Sometimes a concomitant is the forcing of characters to act out of character in order to serve the exigencies of the story.
- Disregard of the principles of narrative viewpoint.
- Mixing genres.
- Wooden and dull characterisation, also uninteresting dialogue heavily weighted with content which fulfils none of the functions of good dialogue.
- A major one: problems with moving characters around, resulting in a compulsion to describe the opening and shutting of every door and similar. Also, too many static scenes in which characters do nothing but sit around talking, often over meals. Prodigious consumption of cups of tea/coffee.
- A worrying lack of awareness of the publishing/bookselling industries, sometimes even of contemporary fiction. Failure to appreciate that merely writing a book which is, in general terms, good enough to be published doesn't by any means ensure that it will be published. The other side of this coin is the aspiring author who sets out deliberately to write the kind of book which s/he thinks will sell and who produces a novel which lacks true emotional commitment on the part of the author.
- Especially where the women's market is concerned, lack of warmth, nobody in the novel you can like.
- A cluster, including: bad writing; disregard or ignorance of the rules of written English; unoriginal ideas and thinking; lack of an individual voice or, disastrously, a dull one; lack of verve, combined with an inclination to focus unrelentingly upon life's miseries.

Golgonooza

Knowing the market appeal of your manuscript and finding a good literary agent are two vital steps for an aspiring novelist seeking a UK publisher. Golgonooza's unique review, award and agent introduction service help you with both.

We are a new company operated by a small and dedicated Editorial team, and powered by a national network of expert freelance bookseller Readers. We created nooza.com because we recognise the increasing difficulties that new writers are faced with when trying to get published.

Mainstream publishers such as HarperCollins, Macmillan, Bloomsbury and Penguin can no longer cope with the number of submissions they receive and advise new writers to only approach them via a literary agent. However getting an agent to represent you or give feedback on your material can often seem an impossible task.

Our expert Reader reviews ensure every submission receives confidential, expert, market-oriented feedback. Our insights on book trends, similar works, and most importantly whether or not a book is likely to interest a UK publisher, could prove invaluable. If it shows serious potential, we'll award a work a Golgonooza Medal of Merit and offer the writer a FREE introduction to top UK literary agents in our online Exhibition.

To submit your novel for review simply register and enter your details. Then login to your new personalised and confidential submission area and start uploading works. (For more details on how to submit go to our Reviews section and click on 'how to submit').

Contact details

Web: *www.nooza.com*
Email: *contact@nooza.com*

Further information

Society of Editors and Proofreaders: *www.sfep.org.uk*

The Society for Editors and Proofreaders (SfEP) is a professional organization based in the UK for editors and proofreaders ñ the people who strive to make text accurate and readable. It aims to promote high editorial standards to achieve recognition of the professional status of its members and associates.

SERVICES YOU MAY REQUIRE:

DIGITAL & POD PRINTING SERVICES

Most self-publishing companies offer a short print run service which is a digital print run. The emergence of this technology has been instrumental in helping a wider range of authors get into print, as historically the only route to print was on a litho press which was horrendously expensive when printing in low numbers. Nowadays, digital printing means you can affordably get a low run of books ie. 25-300 at a reasonable price.

One criticism levelled at digital printing is the curious dislike of the higher quality paper. Traditionalists in the publishing and bookselling industry say that the thicker, brighter quality of the paper is a sure-fire indication of digital printing, which in turn infers self-publishing, which in turn switches some people off.

Developments in technology have enabled books to exist only virtually until they are ordered – print-on-demand. Within 48 hrs, a good print-on-demand printer can have a book printed and ready for despatch. There are a number of printers who offer this service (listed under DIGITAL & POD PRINTERS on page 218). There are also self-publishing companies who offer the publishing services with a print-on-demand print solution (listed under POD PUBLISHERS see page 218).

Developments in technology have enabled books to exist only virtually until they are ordered. They are then printed on demand (hence the name!). Within 48 hrs, a good print-on-demand printer can have a book printed and ready for despatch. There are a number of printers who offer this service.

Advantages of print-on-demand

- Print-on-demand comes into its own in a number of areas:
    - on low-selling titles
    - reprinting out-of-print titles
    - selling online in the international marketplace
- It is the most ecological way to produce hardcopy reading matter.
- It is a cost effective way to do low print runs, with no minimum and no maximum print run order
- There are no storage fees
- There are no "small order" or "low selling" distribution fees
- Your book never goes out of print
- You can use book proofs for marketing purposes
- It is far more ecological – and this is one of the biggest benefits to today's world and not one to be taken lightly
- You can make changes

The main disadvantages of POD

- It is very difficult to sell 2,000 books even when 'hand-selling' them (ie. face-to-face meetings, personal contacts, book tours, events, talks, signings and general trudging the streets). It is much harder again when relying on the internet. You will need to spend money on online advertising which becomes costly and is more of a scatter-gun approach. Statistics quoted at the outset of this book confirmed that few readers buy books in response to an advertisement.
- You don't see the quality before it is sold. Does it remain consistent, or, like most things in this world, does the quality die off after a time?

- The main disadvantage of POD is the price structure. The POD companies price these types of books 10-20% higher than traditional publishing and whilst price isn't always the primary determinant for choosing whether to buy a book, it is a significant factor when the author is unknown.

With POD, it is critical to do the maths and set Set the price of the book accordingly

A cost example from an online POD Company – Lulu:
To produce my romantic fiction title averaging around 220 pages on 8.5 x 11" size perfect bound, I am quoted $8.93 (see page 228) which is around £6.00 per book (on an approximate 66% exchange rate). I therefore need to sell it at £8.00 on Lulu to make any profit. Given that Lulu only sells via its own website, I would need to promote my book on Amazon Advantage which commands a 60% royalty, leaving the author with 45%. Even at a higher than average cover price, I still stand to make no money. Quite the opposite in fact:

Retail price	£9.99
Less Amazon Advantage discount of 60%	- £5.99
Money returned to author/publisher	£4.00
Cost to print the book	£6.00
Profit/loss per book	**- £2.00**

This calculation illustrates the fact that authors need to price the title above comparative books, or pay for the honour of producing and selling their book. Most POD titles have a RRP of £12.95 upwards which makes new authors less accessible or desirable.

A cost example from a UK-based POD printer –

Antony Rowe:

It is important to shop around, and Antony Rowe are a reputable UK-based printer. For the same book as above, Antony Rowe quote £3.00 per book, which means that I am left with some (albeit small) profit on the highest possible middleman discount.

Retail price	£9.99
Less Amazon Advantage discount of 60%	- £5.99
Money returned to author/publisher	£4.00
Cost to print the book	£3.00
Profit/loss per book	+ **£1.00**

This is clearly a much better avenue. Antony Rowe make titles available in the UK via all the standard channels and if you sell direct to the end-consumer or to a bookshop, you will get much better percentages.

Some helpful tips and cautions when printing on demand:

- Get reassurances on production values – the quality of the paper, the binding, consistency of reproduction etc as you rarely see the book orders as they are despatched.
- Get guarantees on price and delivery lead-time
- Ensure the title is correctly listed with all book data and website listings, as the book will not be for sale in shops. Accuracy is the difference between sales and no sales.
- Ensure your contract includes your right to terminate the agreement with a maximum of one month's notice.
- Limit licences to 1-2 years, so you can review your options after this test-market period, and POD rights should never be licensed to a third party without your agreement.
- Most POD sell your book through their online shop and grant you 10% royalties on each title sold. Alternatively,

you can set up your own website and retain 100% of royalties.

- Find out how much you can buy books for; remember that you don't gain any economies of scale over time when books are printed and fulfilled incrementally. The cost per unit (ie. the profit margin) won't change.
- If reprinting out-of-print titles, be sure that all rights have reverted to you and get the original publisher's agreement if the book was first published less than 25 years ago.

The Society of Authors (www.societyofauthors.net) provide a helpful section in the Publications section on their website which discusses POD in a bit more depth

COMPANIES OFFERING DIGITAL PRINTING SERVICES

There are many companies offering print-on-demand services, and again I have just taken a selection from an internet search. Whilst I have worked with some, such as Antony Rowe, others I haven't but have heard positive comment about them. Again the descriptions of what is offered are the companies' own.

Antony Rowe

Antony Rowe is one of the best known short- to medium-run book manufacturers in the UK. We bring our pioneering approach to every project and to every stage of the process - from pre-press right through to delivery.

We can print your book to order with absolutely no barriers on quantity. Single copies or ultra-short-runs of 10s, 20s, 30s can be produced cost-effectively. Per unit, it'll cost just the same.

We store all our books in a ready-to-print digital format, so you won't need to warehouse it, worry about it going out of print, or pulp copies that don't sell. By joining forces with Gardners Books, Britain's largest book wholesalers, we've also given our customers unique access to the UK's biggest distribution and ordering network. Gardners have access to hundreds of thousands of specialist and hard to find titles. Yours could be one of them. This makes marketing, selling and distributing your book that much easier.

What's more, we can now offer you a cost-effective way into the biggest marketplace of them all, the United States. All we need is your electronic file. We'll send it over the Atlantic where our US partner will print and deliver your book anywhere in the country.

Contact details:
Phone: 01323 500040
Email: *bob.hunt@antonyrowe.co.uk*
Web: *www.antonyrowe.co.uk*

Lightning Source

Lightning Source is a recognized leader in the print-on-demand industry, having printed more than 5.0 million books for more than 1,800 publishers around the world. Lightning Source's digital library currently holds more than 100,000 orderable titles and is growing by an average of 400 titles per week. Publishers storing their titles in our library will be able to reach a broader audience at virtually no risk.

While we are a fairly new company, we are also a subsidiary of a long-standing industry leader. We bring to the table all of the worldwide benefits and strengths of Ingram's heritage. We are flexible, open to ideas and believe in keeping the process easy to manage.

Publishers can choose whether to makes books available to the US or UK markets, or both. You then supply the digital files for print on demand or ebook products or, if a digital file is not available, one copy of each book for print on demand titles. All ebook titles must be submitted digitally. Publishers retain the rights to these titles and Lightning Source handles everything else in the process:

- we electronically store the books. You can determine whether these books will be available in hardcover, trade paperback and/or eBook.
- as a publisher, when you need a particular book, you simply send an order to Lightning Source via the web. We will deliver what you want, whatever the quantity, when you need it. The average turnaround time for publisher ordered print-on-demand titles in paperback is 5 days and in hardback 12 days.

Lightning Source UK have recently won the award for Innovation in Publishing 2005 at the Print Media Management Quality in Production Conference on Thursday 19th May. We were recommended for the award by South Bank University Press.

"Lightning Source has helped London South Bank University keep its back catalogue alive and to market test the demand for new works at a low cost, due to the innovative way they publish. This helps to keep low-demand specialist books on print for years to come and build new markets for both new and experienced publishers." *Alan Lee, Document Services Manager, London South Bank University Press.*

Contact details:
Phone: +44 (0) 1908 443555
Email: enquiries@lightningsource.co.uk
Web: www.lightningsource.com

RPM Print & Design

We print a vast range of commercial literature including brochures, catalogues, leaflets, stationery and much more. We can combine traditional offset litho and digital printing to give the most cost-effective solutions and arrange for mailshots to be despatched direct to your target audience.

We offer a complete service in short run book production service that is ideal for proof copies, test marketing and bringing backlist titles back into production. Perfect bound and case bound options are available.

For the self-publisher, RPM offer a design and illustration service as well as an editorial referral service. We have also recently launched our new twice-yearly magazine "Self publisher" which is also on our website.

Contact details:
Phone: 01243 787077
Email: *sales@rpm-repro.co.uk*
Web: *www.rpm-repro.co.uk*

LONG PRINT RUN

Long print runs are done on litho-presses and are expensive for short runs. Real economies of scale kick in at 1000-2000+ but that is a LOT of books to store in your house. If you are going to do a big print run then clear a wall or room in a dry area ie. not in a damp shed, or sign up with a wholesaler who will warehouse your books and fulfil orders (see page 188).

Further information

British Printing Industries Federation:
www.britishprint.com
The British Printing Industries Federation is the principal business support organisation for the UK print, printed packaging and graphic communication industry and is one of this country's leading trade associations. This website connects to a separate one, *www.selectprinter.com* where you can find a range of printers local to you and/or relevant to your needs.

SERVICES YOU MAY REQUIRE: E-PUBLISHING

One area little talked about in the industry is e-publishing. This isn't because it doesn't count. It does. It is a rapidly changing feast, and the information below is a snapshot of where we are today. By the time the second edition of this book comes out in January 2007, the picture will look very different.

Analysis of e-publishing

Currently, e-publishing is a choice based on audience. Not everyone embraces technology very quickly and you will limit your audience too much if your book depends on the non-techno-bods buying it. Therefore, most people who have their head up and eyes open will choose to co-produce their book both as a hard-copy edition and an e-book. However, if your text is aimed at an audience of techno-bods, then you can safely just e-publish and not worry about hard-copy publication.

Benefits of e-publishing

- It's light – digital content doesn't require warehouse space or an intricately inefficient system of handling returns.
- Competitive pricing – printing in small runs makes it difficult to keep prices competitive, but if you're not even turning on the printing presses, that's no longer a problem.
- Disintermediation – the e-publishing buzzword. E-publishing allegedly has the potential to cut out all the middlemen or intermediaries – the distributors, wholesalers, bookstores, printers etc so that customers deal directly with the author.

- Can build and change content with ease
- More interactive – can add hyperlinks to eg. glossary of references, index, include art & video etc
- Full text search and fast delivery – will always trump paging through the back of a book for something technical
- WebScriptions makes partial works of authors available, something that was never possible before.
- E-books are more permanent. Most publishers see a book's launch as a one year period; if it fails to sell, then the book is remaindered. E-books last longer without taking up 'space'.

Reticence to e-publishing

- The only group resistant to e-books is consumers. Many consumers, never having actually seen or touched a dedicated e-reader before, mistakenly think that the only way to read an e-book is on your computer or cell phone; and currently there is no price advantage once retailer discounting comes into play.
- Poor screen quality, limited battery power and damage-sensitive ie don't get it wet.
- It's also hard for consumers to wade through the mess of incompatible formats. Although PDF e-books are ubiquitous, their print-ready formatting makes them ill-suited for e-book readers.
- E-books solve only one part of the issues facing authors, that of distribution. But there are still two very important areas not addressed - marketing and editing. Unless this new world of Amazon includes an editing service and some sort of marketing that makes sense, it can never come close to the current publishing world. Until then, e-books remain a niche product for niche markets that don't warrant the full hassle of a publishing house.
- E-books are difficult to trade

- Not physical - the comfort derived from tactile manipulation of a physical book and its pages is not found with ebooks.
- Not convenient - requires new book purchasing, organizing and reading (e.g. bookmarking) habits.
- Not visible - browsing for books in a bookstore appeals to people.
- Ebook readers are expensive and technology dates quickly
- Digital rights management (see below)
- Pricing strategy (see below)

Developments that enhance e-publishing

- Backend content management systems are becoming more robust and easier for ecommerce companies to maintain
- Content creators are becoming more comfortable with handling the tasks of designing and formatting (just look at the diversity of layouts in weblogs).
- Independent content creators are ready for do-it-yourself ebook solutions, and big publishers would like nothing more than a way to kill the aftermarket, and selling ebooks would do precisely that. As with iTunes, nothing goes out of print or stock. Copyright owners could potentially have more flexibility about setting the price of content over the duration of the copyright and not have to compete against resellers. Comes into its own for certain types of books ie computer books.

Pricing strategies

In theory, pricing strategies vary – small independently published books price low in order to gain audience; mss-market titles start high and just keep reducing till it sells.

In reality, there are currently no standards, although many e-book buyers expect it to be cheaper because of the lack of tangible production process ie. current expectations are 75% off hard-copy price for fiction and 60% off the hard-copy price for non-fiction. The argument is that nobody has to actually print, warehouse, or ship physical books.

But there's always a cost. There's always a middleman taking his cut. And above all, your text has a VALUE. Everyone wants something for nothing nowadays, and the only people who sell something for nothing seem to be authors.

Authors need to take control of this. The 'value' of your book should remain the same; maybe you might choose to offer discounts at certain periods of time or in certain volume sales ie. 25-35% off the hard-copy price. You need to work out how much time and cost has gone into the project, what you need to earn out of it and work back from there in order to set your price.

The new author is the invariably the loser in the publishing process currently (unless you hit the big time quickly, but many don't). There are too many books being created and in the future fewer books will sell in excess of1000 copies – as there is just too much choice! The author never stands to make any money from his writing unless he takes control of the process.

**As an author, your text has a VALUE,
not just a price!**

Doing the maths

- Assume the average work of non-fiction takes 6 months to research, write and secure all permissions/copyrights, typeset and produce to finished standard (and this is a very optimistic time frame!).
- Assume the book will sell around 1000 (at this level, the demand for this book is saturated).

- Assume an author would like to earn a reasonable £20,000 per year equivalent from his six months hard labour ie. £10,000 for six months work – which is paltry in comparison to many other lines of work.
- In paperback, this book would sell for £12.99; of which the author would see approximately £2 after bookseller / distributor percentage, print and P&P cost. If he sells all 1000 copies, he has made £2,000 for his six months work.
- As an e-book, he has to:
  - o create a website, host, promote, link, advertise etc and although he gets 100% of book-price, he has put a lot of budget and time in to the website
  - o upload to other sites like Amazon, where he pays a percentage to them for every sale he makes
  - o manage with website and keep it "live"

Example calculation

Hard-copy price	£12.99
Market demands e-book price at 65% less	£4.55
Selling 500 through website nets him	£2,275.00
Cost of website (very conservative!!)	- £1,500.00
Cost of hosting & advertising	- £ 500.00
Profit through direct sales:	*£ 275.00*
Selling 500 through Amazon at £4.55	£2,275.00
Amazon 55% discount	£1,252.00
Profit through Amazon sales	*£1,023.75*
Total profit:	**£1,298.00**

This is a very paltry sum indeed for 6 months hard work, actual investment, the dedication to getting it out there etc. All this effort so that someone can have the benefit of your life's work for £4.55. The profit of £1,298 barely pays for the electricity and phone bills and the endless cups of coffee it took for you to write the damn thing.

The text is worth more than £4.55 irrespective of whether you have to print or not. Those in favour of cheap e-books argue that you sell more. But if every book was discounted to this level, the market would just get saturated faster. Human beings only have a finite amount of time to read, and there are already too many reading materials out on the market.

Ultimately, how you price your book is up to you; the strategy should be to cover your costs as quickly as possible; e-book retailers must realize e-books and paper versions are very different animals, not just differently priced ones. There are other costs involved which also need to be covered, and the principle of e-book retailing is to help authors take control of the selling process.

Following the same line of calculation as above, but based on the author selling his e-book for £12.99, he stands to make approximately £7,417. This is still a small sum, but at least it is more reasonable. Maybe after selling the first 1000 and recouping the initial investment, you can reduce the price. Or maybe you will choose to sell at 25% less than hard-copy price and hope to sell 2,000, thus still recouping your costs. As the retailer, it is up to you.

e-publishing is a way for authors to take control

Is e-publishing a reality?

Some believe yes, others believe no. The Society of Authors believes it is not a profitable enterprise either now or in the foreseeable future.

People have been predicting e-books and e-book readers for at least two decades, but this past year marked two watershed moments in the e-book world. From the e-book reader perspective, a grayscale e-book reader (Ebookwise 1150) began selling near the $100 range, and a high-end reader (Cybook) capable of reading most e-book formats began selling near the $400 range. Both devices allow importing of .txt, .rtf and .html files. Amazon.com's buying of Mobipocket signals that it is poised to support and promote a single e-book format. It also could mean that Amazon.com's POD service (Booksurge) will start designing and publishing e-books for formats other than PDF.

But more importantly, in America there has been a significant shift of educational and academic texts being downloaded under short-term licences. This could signify the beginning of a whole new way of educational texts being bought which would have a major impact on the industry.

Here are a few things to look out for as the e-book market emerges:

1. Are e-book software companies continuing to sell reasonably-priced client applications to produce e-books? (Right now, Mobipocket Publishing Standard Edition costs $150). If these client applications are abandoned, or if the prices go up significantly, that could be a sign that the software company (and accompanying web distribution site) are wrapping the formatting magic into the server product. That's bad for content creators because it allows the publishing/distribution channel to "own" the tools for layout and design.

2. Will the number of e-book file formats increase or decrease? Maintaining this many versions of the same content would add significantly to the time, cost and aggravation of self-publishing.

How to publish an e-book

Firstly, bear in mind that printers such as Antony Rowe produce e-books as well as print-on-demand and short print runs. If you are keen to do it yourself, however, you convert the book to the following languages to ensure easy digital access. E-publishing is not standardised as yet and therefore there are a number of ways to read and download:

- PDF, XML and OEB (Open e-book – an internet language based on HTML and XML); these formats can be read on notebook computers, Palm Pilots and many e-book readers
- LIT is a Microsoft programme with Cleartype™ which sharpens LCD screens; this can be read on MS Reader with Cleartype™

Making it available for sale

- create your own website and promote it to relevant groups
- upload to Amazon, B&N, BookLocker
- put onto a CD which is a searchable format and have live hyperlinks.

For fiction, many people will put the first chapter onto their website as a free read. For non-fiction, it is better to put 'sound-bites' from each chapter to give an overview of the content of the book.

Digital Rights Management (DRM)

Digital rights management is an issue under close scrutiny by the top dogs in the industry. I am not going to get bogged down by DRM in this book as it is such a rapidly changing feast. Suffice it to say that a major issue surrounding e-books is the "problem" of anti-piracy and digital rights management. Many of the e-book industry supporters say that commercial interests will pretty much guarantee that e-book devices will employ some kind of DRM.

SUMMARY

- The publisher is always the primary investor behind a book. As a self-publisher, that is YOU. If you don't get behind it 100%, then nobody else will.
- Plan the process out properly. Schedule the time in properly; follow industry standard procedures and set a realistic publication date. Don't rush it and miss out important parts of the process.
- The cover, including design, synopsis and reviews, combines to make 74% of the decision-making process to buy a book. Take the time and expertise to get it right.
- Use your local bookshop to research as much as possible.
- Maximise the places where you register and catalogue your book. Exploit all opportunities for customers to find your book.
- In this modern day of computerised information, one small error is the difference between your book being located on a digital search and not. Name your book wisely and ensure you put the information in correctly.
- Understand the maths. As a publisher, you are a businessman and must take a business-like approach. Behave as though you have to account for every penny spent and report to someone for all income or incoming shortfalls!
- There is only one price – the one that has enough profit to make it worthwhile yet is low enough to make it sell. Don't ever sell for less than it costs to produce!!
- The real drawback to independently self-publishing is the lack of guarantee. The author has no contract with any one company that guarantees to deliver a book to a certain, pre-agreed standard within an agreed time frame to an agreed budget.

For further information:

Nielsen BookData : *www.bookdata.co.uk*
Book Data is the leading supplier of content-rich bibliographic information about English-language books to booksellers and libraries in the UK and worldwide, bringing together information about books and other published media from around the world.

Bowker : *www.bowkerlink.com*
Founded in 1872, Bowker is the official US agency for assigning ISBNs and is North Americaís leading provider of bibliographic information.
The **BowkerLink**[a] system provides publishers with an easy-to-use automated tool to update or add to their listings in Bowkerís databases. Publishers may also view and update their publisher contact information.

PubEasy: *www.pubeasy.com*
The Global Publishing e-Marketplace, representing new standards in e-commerce for the global bookselling industry.

Book Industry Communications : *www.bic.org.uk*
Book Industry Communication (BIC) is the book trade standards body. BIC's website includes trade standards for Product Information, EDI and barcoding as well as many research reports on aspects of book trade e-commerce and the standards infrastructure for digital publishing.

British Printing Industries Federation : *www.britishprint.com*
The British Printing Industries Federation is the principal business support organisation for the UK print, printed packaging and graphic communication industry and is one of this country's leading trade association.

PART V

SELF-PUBLISHING SERVICES COMPANIES

The purpose of this chapter is to analyse the services offered by self-publishing companies to help authors make their own evaluation. The evaluation assesses 19 companies in total and these sub-divide into companies who Full Services which invariably result in the production of a short (or long) print run of books, and companies that offer POD production.

INTRODUCING THE EVALUATION

There are some 15–20 self-publishing services companies that regularly come up on Google or advertise in the press. Some are UK based, some are US companies operating within the UK. They all have different services and different ways of expressing what they offer, and it will take the independent author quite a while to establish who offers exactly what they want, so I have done the work for you.

In order to make an evaluation and experience the different businesses from the author perspective, I submitted the same 62,000 word manuscript to all of the companies offering self-publishing services. I did this under a pseudonym. I didn't think the book was too bad, apart from the title which was rubbish (Wild Goose Chase), and I was trying something different, trying to blend a travelogue with a fictional story. It didn't work, as confirmed to me by an independent editor whose judgement I respect. Having requested an independent editor's report, I had a standard against which I could judge all responses.

It is worth noting here that quotes often varied based on their assessment of potential page count, which ranged from 176 pages to 230 pages. Their recommended format size also varied.

I didn't send it to the ones who quoted fees and services on their website without sight of a manuscript as this would have just wasted everyone's time. For this latter group of people, sight of my manuscript was not going to change their quotation to me.

CAVEAT: this is a snapshot taken in 2005, and the scene changes very, very quickly. In the last 3 months, since I set the wheels in motion to do this assessment, 3-4 new self-publishing services companies have already entered the market, and some of the services offered by existing companies have changed. So once you know the basics, it is still worth approaching individual companies to find out what has changed.

By 2006, it will have changed again and I am confident that I will be publishing, either in hardcopy or online, annual updates – particularly if you register your interest on my website - www.indepublishing.com.

FULL SERVICE COMPANIES

There is little standardisation and clarity in the industry, so I have chosen the following criteria to assess their offer:

- Design
- Editing
- Proof-reading
- Production & printing
- Registrations
- Royalties
- Book pricing
- Free copies
- Distribution
- Marketing
- Reprinting

Full service companies evaluated:

- Able Publishing
- Amherst Publishing
- Amolibros
- Ashridge Press
- Better Book Company
- Book Guild
- Matador
- Pen Press Publishers

Able Publishing : www.ablepublishing.co.uk
Short print run book production company

Literature
High quality books and the author retains creative control on content, format and quantities. The parent company was an educational publisher, and having published their own material, they then moved on to helping other authors to self-publish around 12 years ago.

Their quote to me was based on Standard B format (128x198mm), 176 page sides plus cover and this came to £2,904 for a short print run of 500 books. These are delivered to you to store, fulfil, sell and invoice; authors retain 100% royalties on sales.

For this price, you get:

- DESIGN: final artwork of an author's cover design and supplied imagery
- EDITING: quote provided depending on requirement; most authors do not wish to have their work edited
- PROOF-READING: quote provided as requested; most authors undertake this themselves.
- PRODUCTION & PRINTING: undertake all origination of cover and typesetting, including advice on production values and liaison with printers.
- REGISTRATIONS: Able can issue one or you can do it yourself, and the barcode is obtained once the cover is designed.
- DISTRIBUTION: limited stock is held by Able for fulfilment to Amazon or direct orders, and they take 35%. Able encourage authors to undertake as much of the distribution/fulfilment themselves in order to retain maximum return. An author's title is also listed on the website, but you cannot buy online from them, and they advise that it is very difficult to get into any of the main bookshops with an unknown title.
- MARKETING: Able believe authors are the best marketers of their own titles and need to understand their market; Able refuse to make false promises about selling books. Therefore they offer limited marketing ie. produce a flyer and mail to author's list of contacts. If they handle any sales, then they take 35% of selling price. They will link from Able Publishing website to author's own, if you have one set up.
- REPRINTING: they do not do print-on-demand, but can organise ongoing print runs at author cost.

- ADDITIONAL SERVICES AVAILABLE: none mentioned; but they do encourage authors to visit for a face-to-face meeting in order to maximise the opportunities

Summary

- A very straightforward, no frills website. The focus remains on the production element of the books rather than the edit and subsequent sales.

Gill Williams and Catherine Williams from Able comment:

We feel that many worthwhile books would not have been produced without companies such as our own, although it remains very difficult to get them stocked in the traditional channels. Certainly addressing the resistance of wholesalers and bookshop suppliers to self-published titles would help many worthwhile books find their audience.

Amherst Publishing Ltd : www.amherstpublishing.co.uk
Specialist writing, publishing and editorial services

Literature
Their quote to me was based on standard B format (128x198mm) and totalled £2,988 for a short print run of 500 books. These are delivered to you, for you to store, fulfil, sell and invoice, and you retain 100% royalties on sales.

For this price, you get:

- DESIGN: final artwork of an author's cover design and supplied imagery.
- EDITING: services available on request and in addition
- PROOF-READING: none mentioned
- PRODUCTION & PRINTING: advice on production values and liaison with printers
- REGISTRATIONS: advise how to get ISBN, barcode and do legal deposits, under your own imprint.
- DISTRIBUTION: none mentioned
- MARKETING: There is a launch services package available for an extra fee, but their literature also provides some basic guidelines.
- REPRINTING: no
- ADDITIONAL SERVICES AVAILABLE: none mentioned

Summary
Amherst is a book production company with editorial services available

Amolibros : www.amolibros.com

A complete self publishing services to authors who wish to avoid getting overburdened by the time-consuming aspects of either or both production and marketing.

Literature

Amolibros offers the complete service to assist self-publishing authors, offering well executed production to suit target market. Amolibros provides you with realistic expectations and professional assistance.

Quote

Their quote to me was based on standard B format (128x198mm), 256 pages which totalled £3,839 for a short print run of 500 books; this includes an additional 100 covers for promotional purposes. The books can be delivered to you, for which you store, fulfil, sell and invoice, and you retain 100% royalties on sales, or you can use their distribution service, see below.

For this price, you get:

- DESIGN: yes
- EDITING: services available on request and in addition
- PROOF-READING: yes
- PRODUCTION & PRINTING: yes
- REGISTRATIONS: produced under author's own imprint; but they organise ISBN, barcode and legal deposits
- DISTRIBUTION: optional; Gazelle take 65% of cover price and Amolibros, as consolidation agent, take 5%
- MARKETING: There are optional marketing services listed, available for an extra fee.
- REPRINTING: no
- ADDITIONAL SERVICES AVAILABLE: audio books

Summary

The price looked high in comparison to the others, but you get what you pay for in this life; this is a fairly comprehensive package in all.

Jane Tatum from Amolibros comments:
Self-publishing is definitely a viable route to market nowadays, particularly as mainstream publishers are increasingly accountancy driven. There is still some distance to go, particularly in terms of publishers who denigrate self-publishing (probably because it is occupying a larger space nowadays!) as well as book reviewers who are too scared to put their reputation on the line by endorsing a book that hasn't been "approved" by a mainstream publisher. As the quality of self-published titles improves, so will the reaction from the publishing and bookselling industries.

Historically there have been some poor quality titles produced by vanity publishers, and sadly self-publishers walk in the footsteps of this reputation. It is a different time now, although I still have a reservations about companies that publish on behalf of self-publishing authors. Authors should never assign copyright to anyone; they should be free to sell any subsidiary rights and should be entitled to 100% royalties of their books up until the time they negotiate a 'sales' deal with a company. I also believe that the author's own logo should appear on the spine as a self-publishing company's logo may prejudice a bookseller against stocking the title.

Seemingly these historic issues are being addressed, and the real changes will need to take place in the supply chain which is complex and multitudinous.

Ashridge Press : www.country-books.co.uk
A comprehensive range of non-fiction titles. A complete service for the self publisher.

Literature

Ashridge offer the complete service for the self-publishing author. Country Books creates books for small publishers and societies, and proudly boasts prize-winners, serialisation and national reviews.

Quote

Their quote to me totalled £1,714 for a short print run of 300 books based on 208 pages (I assume standard format). I guess another 200 books would take the quote near the £2000 mark. These are delivered to the author, for you to store, fulfil, sell and invoice; you retain 100% royalties. Authors own the books and the copyright completely.

For this price, you get:

- DESIGN: included in price; if authors want to design independently, Ashridge will put them in touch with a printer, but take no percentage
- EDITING: a pool of freelance editors to ensure the manuscript is sent to the right type of editor
- PROOF-READING: yes
- PRODUCTION & PRINTING: yes
- REGISTRATIONS: produced under author's own imprint or Ashridge imprint; will optionally organise ISBN, barcode and legal deposits irrespective of whose imprint. Advises Nielsen and Bowker.
- DISTRIBUTION: no, but they can send a list of UK distributors for authors to set up own accounts. Can send covers to wholesalers, but caveats this with the fact they take 55-65%.
- MARKETING: no, but can send covers to Nielsen and major libraries accounts, and has accounts with the main chains.
    - No percentage charge for sales; deducts postage at cost for bookshop orders less trade discount - 35% most shops including Waterstones and Ottakars; 42.5% WH Smith; 25% Bertrams; 35% Gardners, Macaula, Holt Jackson, etc.
    - Has previously secured features for books and one author won the Lichfield Literary Prize.

   - Advises that poetry is a notoriously poor seller; surprising titles, however, can do very well. He will decline manuscripts that have no chance of sales.
- REPRINTING: ongoing print runs under Ashridge imprint (rate tbc)
- ADDITIONAL SERVICES AVAILABLE: none mentioned

Summary

It's refreshing to see someone shouting about their credentials, which speaks louder than a booklet on services. Little reference is made about the process, but in this case I assume it to be because the owner is a genuine old-school publisher who doesn't see that the author needs to worry about that, because he will do what it takes.

The Better Book Company : www.better-book.co.uk
Publishers, Self-publications, Book designers & printers, Marketing & distribution

Their literature / website advises that the editor works with author to produce a really good looking book. They will consider an author's cover designs, but reserve the right to revise/reject. The author retains all foreign, TV and film rights.

Quote
To produce a B format paperback of 230 pages x 500 books will be £3,975. For this price, you get:

- DESIGN: yes, you work closely with an editor through the process, who can advise on all production requirements including title and price
- EDITING: copyedit yes; in depth editing will be charged as extra
- PROOF-READING: tbc
- PRODUCTION & PRINTING: fully typeset into Quark Express ready for final print. Price includes two sets of print proofs for author final approval; quote charges for a set quantity of books which are delivered to you upon printing.
- REGISTRATIONS: produced under author's own imprint; and they advise how to obtain ISBN and issue legal deposits. They supply the barcode.
- DISTRIBUTION: no, but they can advise on this; will be displayed on Amazon & store databases automatically if you have an ISBN.
- MARKETING: marketing advice only; your title will feature on the company's website
- ROYALTIES: All sales revenue goes directly to the author; copyright and sales rights belong to the author in all media and countries.
- REPRINTING: can be quoted and price met by author
- ADDITIONAL SERVICES AVAILABLE: none mentioned

Summary
Nicely produced literature; friendly company and solid offer.

The Book Guild Ltd : www.bookguild.co.uk
The independent publishers

Literature:
A truly comprehensive service including all marketing and distribution, including Bookseller bi-annual Buyers Guides, wholesalers and library suppliers. Reassurance of quality is provided by a beautifully produced, glossy catalogue with great book jackets and well-written book descriptions and author information.

Quote:
They have a range of alternative services which span (i) production only (ii) sponsored publishing and (iii) commissioned publishing. I was quoted under the Commissioned Publishing offer.

Their quote to me totalled £8,800 for a short print run of 500 hard-back books. They recommend a retail price of £16.99. The author receives between 20 – 50 free copies depending on payment structure of fees.

For this price, you get:
- DESIGN: full design service
- EDITING: Copy edit, with advice on structure and pace; also write the back jacket text at this point.
- PROOF-READING: yes
- PRODUCTION & PRINTING: yes
- REGISTRATIONS: they obtain ISBN, register the title with Nielsen Bookdata and issue legal deposits
- DISTRIBUTION: Seem to be very comprehensive, and inclusive in price; aimed at book chains, wholesalers and library suppliers
- MARKETING: Seem to be very comprehensive; inclusive in price is a Sales Manager selling only Book guild titles as well as a stand at the London Book Fair.
- REPRINTING: yes
- ROYALTIES: are calculated at 30% of the published price and paid every six months. Contracts are for a 2 year duration and authors receive any unsold copies back at the end of this time as copyright is always held by the author
- ADDITIONAL SERVICES AVAILABLE: Selling paperback and other rights

Summary

- Firstly, Book Guild offer a variety of different ‘contracts depending on the marketability of an author/title
- They were over double the price of the next most expensive quote on the same number of copies. However on closer inspection, this is because of the sheer volume of services which includes all ongoing, full editing, design, marketing, sale of paperback / serialisation rights and reprinting. Not to mention the first run is in hardback.
- I questioned the need for hard-back – as an unknown author of a romantic fiction, but I was reassured that this enable sale of paperback rights, although this isn’t a *given* for all books.
- They questioned elements of my manuscript which the independent editor had questioned, which is a real positive.
- They also pay the cost for future print runs; this is a positive as much as it is rare.

Carol Biss of Book Guild comments:

We have always called ourselves commissioned publishers – we are commissioned by the author to perform every single function that a publishing house does. It is a true partnership in so much as it is imperative that we sell the books in order to provide all the services we do. It is therefore a true partnership with the author.

Book Guild’s advice to self-publishing authors:

“Be sure you can afford it: if you recoup your financial investment, consider it a bonus.
Visit the publisher’s office if at all possible.
See samples of the publisher’s latest books.
Ascertain that they have in-house publicity staff.
Ask to see review coverage on current books.
Ascertain that they have proper distribution facilities.
Don’t simply take the cheapest offer: this is a field in which quality counts and costs.
Don’t focus on fame and fortune; just enjoy the experience.”

Matador: www.troubador.co.uk

The complete range of services to authors who want to publish their own book. Matador is just one imprint of Troubador, who publish a range of academic, trade and specialist titles.

Literature

Matador undertake as much or as little of the publishing process as you wish, with a full range of services available. They produce your book to a high standard with the infrastructure to get your book into bookshops.

Quote

Their quote, after sight and due consideration of the manuscript, was based on demi-format (216x138); 220 pages. This totalled £1960 for 500 copies.

For this price, you get:

- DESIGN: artwork from image supplied, or up to £250 for a bespoke cover (depending on complexity)
- EDITING: copy-edit inclusive; other levels available and quoted upon individual need.
- PROOF-READING: included, but authors are requested to read the text plus an additional third pair of eyes.
- PRODUCTION & PRINTING: yes
- REGISTRATIONS: either Author-own or Matador.
- PRICING: Author sets price based on cost per unit and advice from Matador
- DISTRIBUTION: Two options:
    - Troubador distributes on behalf of author and takes 15% off cover price on anything sold. Matador charge a one-off fee of £300 to cover AI's, press release and media co-ordination, and we supply Gardners, Bertrams, THE and 19 library wholesalers. The books belong 100% to the author.
    - Distribution via Gazelle. Matador charge a one-off fee of £300 to cover AI's, press release and media co-ordination which Troubador distributes; but Gazelle use these to sell into retail outlets for which they take 75%. This route is only encouraged when print run is large enough to get economies of scale (1000+).
- ONLINE DISTRIBUTION: 24 hr delivery from Amazon; can make selected titles available with Amazon.com on request, but needs a set-up fee of £100)

- ROYALTIES from net receipts are paid (85% or 25% depending on distribution agreement) 120 days after they have been sold in order to pass on only firm sales.
- MARKETING: £300 for basic package; optional extras (launches, leaflets, postcards etc) agreed in advance
- REPRINTING: quotation supplied before an author commits. If a book is selling well, it might transfer onto a 'partnership' or 'part-funded' arrangement.
- ADDITIONAL SERVICES AVAILABLE: none per se, but Matador is very flexible and seeks to help authors in a variety of different ways.

Summary

Very professional website and literature; links to an independent publisher is a positive. Obviously benefits from good distribution through their links with Troubador. Comprehensive service at a reasonable price, and I liked the Newsflash on website.

Jeremy Thompson of Matador comments:

I have real concern about POD and profitability. Authors must rigorously do the maths, especially when selling print-on-demand digital copies via the trade. The figures don't stack up and authors often don't realise this until they are out of pocket. I urge new authors to follow the structure of calculation as set out in this book (see Setting the Price).

We also find quality is still an issue with some self-published titles which reflects poorly on self-publishing across the board. Quality standards need to be set, and authors can enforce this by requesting a sample copy of a book before signing an agreement.

Pen Press Publishers: www.penpress.co.uk
The real alternative to mainstream publishing – we empower authors to test the market with quality books that compete effectively

Literature
Comprehensive literature offering three service levels and a flexible approach, demonstrating a wide range of titles previously published.

Quote
The quote was based on a paid-for, no-obligation reader's report which provided me with a comprehensive critique. They offer several service levels – (i) Private Editions (ii) Pen Press imprint (iii) Indepenpress imprint. Based on the Pen Press imprint, I was quoted £2,950 for my 62,000 word manuscript.

For this price, you get:

- DESIGN: bespoke or artworking your ideas; both inclusive
- EDITING: copy-edit inclusive; other levels available and quoted upon individual need.
- PROOF-READING: additional at £15 per hour
- PRODUCTION & PRINTING: yes
- REGISTRATIONS: yes
- DISTRIBUTION: online and via Gardners
    - Special Editions: you own all books printed, retain all royalties and manage all sales and distribution
    - Pen Press: competitively-produced titles distributed via Gardners and online
    - Indepenpress: structural edits, proof-reading, researched design, full marketing and enhanced distribution with sales reps presentations
- MARKETING: local marketing launch included, together with Business Cards to hand out; Advanced Marketing available at £35 per hour
- REPRINTING: yes (not for Private Editions)
- ADDITIONAL SERVICES AVAILABLE:
    - marketing services
    - reader's report
    - proof-reading
    - promotional materials (postcards, flyers, posters)
    - small stand at London Book Fair

Summary

Very comprehensive service to suit the many varied needs of authors, charging appropriately for the different service levels required. The Indepenpress imprint enables authors to relaunch under this once sales pass the 1000 mark to exploit industry standard practices.

Lynn Ashman of Pen Press comments:

The self-publishing industry is coming of age. I firmly believe that most authors will turn to self-publishing over the coming years and increasingly publishers and/or agents will pick them up once the author has a proven market.

In order to mature, there are changes still to be made both within the self-publishing industry and the publishing industry overall. What is of paramount importance in the immediate future is that self-publishing companies ensure clarity on offer and authors understand what they should expect to receive.

EVALUATION (CONTINUED)

PRINT-ON-DEMAND PUBLISHING COMPANIES

Publishers of a print-on-demand offer have a different range of criteria from the full services companies:

- Design
- Editing
- Proof-reading
- Production & printing
- Registrations
- Royalties
- Book pricing
- Free copies
- Distribution
- Marketing

Companies offering print-on-demand publishing:

- Authorhouse
- Authorsonline
- Booksurge
- Diadem books
- Lulu
- Planetree publishing
- Publish and be damned (pabd)
- Publish britannica
- Trafford
- Writersservices
- Writersworld

AuthorHouse: www.authorhouse.co.uk
Your voice in print

Authors retain creative control and all rights. Authors are given a personal, knowledgeable advisor. It's a print-on-demand offer, and your final book will be available to order via UK/US distributors and via AuthorHouse online store, and powerful marketing tools are available for the promotion of book.

Print-on-demand offer:

- DESIGN: draft your own cover layout and they will artwork
- EDITING: none included; submit unformatted manuscript in digital or hard-copy for them to set
- PROOF-READING: none offered
- PRODUCTION & PRINTING: £605 for 62,000 words
- REGISTRATIONS: ISBN registration costs £70
- PRICE: I set the price within a range based on the wordcount.
- FREE COPIES: if I publish, contract and pay for the services in August I will get 5 free copies
- ROYALTIES: Authors get 25% of cover price total per sale; you need to check if you set the price, or they do.
- DISTRIBUTION: title becomes available to more than 25,000 retail outlets and internet retailers, as well as via AuthorHouse online store
    - UK distribution: they list the book with Gardners for print-on-demand orders, and bookstores can order it upon demand
    - US distribution: they list the book with Bertrams & Ingrams for POD orders, and bookstores can order it in upon demand.
- MARKETING: no, but you can optionally buy a booksigning or marketing kit for £230, and for £60 get a domain name (*NB. Just a domain; not content provision or website hosting).*
- REPRINTING: pay per book; cost per unit never decreases
- ADDITIONAL SERVICES AVAILABLE: US promotional services

Summary

- The reference to authors retaining all rights is misleading to the new author, because it means copyright (which all authors retain unless otherwise negotiated). It doesn't mean authors retain 100% of royalty percentage.
- It looks like a solid POD offer, and they have some recognisable authors such as Luke Rhinehart (*The Diceman*).

AuthorsOnline Ltd : www.authorsonline.co.uk
Publishing for the 21st Century
Print-on-demand offer

Literature

AuthorsOnline are the new face of self-publishing using new POD technology worldwide distribution via mail order. The website offers news features announcing author successes and a scrolling Latest Books window, which is good.

Quote

All they need to be able to quote is a synopsis and a couple of sample chapters for evaluation. Authors supply the manuscript on disk, CD or email, and the contract is offered only after payment. There are two service levels available to create one master version of my 62,000 word work of fiction into a book, see below.

Their print-on-demand service includes:

- DESIGN: Optional extra for standard service at £350; included within Enhanced service.
- EDITING: Optional extra for standard service at £350; included within Enhanced service.
- PROOF-READING: not included
- PRODUCTION & PRINTING:
- Standard: £700; includes 5 free books to author
- Enhanced: £1,450; includes 20 free books to author
- SHORT PRINT RUN AVAILABILITY? tbc
- REGISTRATIONS: ISBN registration costs £17.62 p/a; assume this includes barcoding; legal deposit is extra £50 for standard service; included in Enhanced service.
- FREE COPIES: as above
- ADDITIONAL COPY COST: per unit cost + 20% (but don't know what per unit cost is).
- ROYALTIES: Author gets 60% of net revenue from retail sales; and AuthorsOnline do all distribution paperwork ie. less bookseller percentage and print costs. Check if you set the selling price, or if they do.
- UK DISTRIBUTION: online distribution available
- US DISTRIBUTION: online distribution available
- MARKETING: services available additionally
- ADDITIONAL SERVICES AVAILABLE:

- All books published and sold as e-books in Adobe Acrobat and MS Reader formats to download from Authors Online website. Authors get 60% of net revenue.
- Post-production alterations are charged at £70.50 per version changed.
- Scanning and insertion of photographs and illustrations are charged at £35.00 per hour
- Online log of all booksales which authors can see for themselves.

Summary

- Being offered a contract AFTER payment is odd
- The inference that you get 60% of royalties is potentially misleading. The inexperienced author will not understand that this means 60% of NET revenues ie. after bookseller discount and print costs.
- Their website is good; it is clearly aimed more at the visiting reader than the visiting potential author which is always a tricky card to play. But the items they choose to put on the home page – Latest Books In, Top Ten Fiction / Non-Fiction and News Stories all interest the reader and reassure the author.
- The caveat to this is that making books available online is a passive selling process; it doesn't necessarily make people aware of your book or product. Unless, of course, you do links, banner ads, regularly update key words on your website and actively become part of the web community – but this all costs.

Booksurge Publishing: www.booksurge.com

It's not about waiting. Wondering. Hoping.
It's about you. A published author. Today.

Website

Booksurge is an online publishing business; owned by Amazon. Their website is extremely modern and new.

Quote

Their quote to me was based on a US size format which is non-standard in the UK (5.25" x 8"), and they set the retail price. In the case of my 62,000 word book, this is set at $15.99 (c. £11.00) and this is not negotiable.

Their print-on-demand service includes:

- DESIGN: templates or final artwork only; bespoke design is $999
- EDITING: Additional charge depending on length of manuscript, $900 up to 75,000 words
    - one to one consultations are $85 per hour
- PROOF-READING: optional; this service is $450
- PRODUCTION & PRINTING: $498 to set and produce
- SHORT PRINT RUN AVAILABILITY? Yes, 300 copies I get at 60% discount off cover price; 500 copies I get 65%; free shipping within the US; shipping to UK tbc
- REGISTRATIONS: ISBN registration & barcode info not provided; US legal deposits yes; UK legal deposit, no information
- FREE COPIES: none
- ROYALTIES: Author gets 25% of online sales; 10% of bookshop sales and 70% of e-book sales. I assume I get 100% of sales if I sell my 500 copies direct?
- UK DISTRIBUTION: double check if onto UK sites
- US DISTRIBUTION: Online; worldwide.
- MARKETING:
    - Amazon Marketplace Management ie. managed fulfilment.
    - Publicity kit $699 includes free strategy meeting, 500 colour postcards; 500 business cards; 500 bookmarks; a professionally written press release and 100 press release inserts
    - OR Marketing Copy Assistance to keep text, author biog and descriptions consistent and clear = $250
    - Press release service for list creation and first release = $399
    - Additional releases to the same list are $99 per distribution

- ADDITIONAL SERVICES AVAILABLE:
  - Author domain service $189 set up & $39 per year (this is registration and hosting only; not content provision). Create link from Booksurge shop to your site
  - Banner ads on Booksurge site - $150 per 3 months
  - Library Sales with a Library of Congress Control number $75
  - Trade Fair package – represent your book at agreed trade shows on the Booksurge stand with 20 books per event; attended booksigning (add cost of printing 50 books), inclusion in Booksurge catalog, rack of cards featuring your book cover, booth space, design & marketing copy for the above ad & promo materials; drayage and shipping costs. Costs $999 for one premier (Book Expo) and two regional/speciality (US based). LBF and Frankfurt are asterisked, but this is not explained. I assume extra charges.

Summary

- I have spent a lot of time on this site, because it looks hopeful when you first enter it. The broken down incremental charges make it look affordable, given that if your book is completely typeset, formatted, registered and designed etc, you can 'produce' it for $99. That's amazingly cheap – or so it seems until you realise that you don't actually get anything for that, except their digital creation of the book in readiness for its first order. Then you only get 25% royalties.
- In effect, you are giving them 75% of the sale of each book to sell through the Booksurge site; but you have to buy hardcopies from them at 60% or so of the cover price – which they set at a high price, and this is not negotiable.
- It is very difficult for individual, unknown titles to be found amongst so many thousands of other books online.
- The inflexibility on the book price is a real problem. Who is going to buy an unknown author? Who will pay £11.00 for romantic fiction – it is well acknowledged that breaking the £10 barrier is a feat in itself? The author should at least have the choice as to what price they wish to sell at. We all know that books retail for far too low a price on the open market, but it is the modern day standard. Until competitive, mainstream published titles are sold for more money, unknown authors cannot overprice themselves.

But when you do the maths in order to get a comparable service to the UK based businesses, it is easy to see why the price has to be high:

$900	for the edit on a 75,000 word book
$999	to design and artwork a bespoke cover
$450	to proof read
$498	for the Author's Advantage Publishing Programme for format the book to my design (assumes I know what I want)
$699	Publicity kit includes free strategy meeting, 500 colour postcards; 500 business cards; 500 bookmarks; a professionally written press release and 100 press release inserts
$399	Press release service for list creation and first release
$99	Additional releases to the same list is per distribution
$4,044	

So for the equivalent of **£3,000** I have an edited, designed, formatted book with press releases and publicity material to an agreed distribution list with one follow up to same list. But I don't actually have a hardcopy of the book for myself for this price. I have to then pay a further **£1,500** to obtain hard copy print outs. Also, being a US-based company, will they charge me to ship these over to the UK?

If I then want any of the desirable extras, I am looking at a further **£1,000** ie:

$306	for the Author domain service including 3 years hosting
?	for content provision – I have to organise this.
$150	for one month of Banner ads on Booksurge site
$75	Library Sales with a Library of Congress Control number
$999	Trade Fair package premier

So, for **£5,500** + website content I can sell my book worldwide. Given that I receive £2.75 of any sale online (only 10% for bookshop order, but let's assume they all sell online for the purposes of calculation), I have to sell 2,000 books just to break even, which is a lot of hard work, particularly when relying on online sales.

Outstanding questions:

I emailed with questions, to which I was still waiting for a response at the time this book went to print:

- If I want a stock of 500 books, I pay a further $2,430. Do I pay for shipping them to the UK?
- Do I get the fully designed and typeset file if I decide to leave Booksurge and print short runs locally?

Diadem Books: www.diadembooks.com
Your affordable gateway to self-publishing and print-on-demand books with unlimited copy editing; POD offer

Literature
They offer unlimited copy editing; on average the book is ready with 90 days. They are a POD company linked with American publisher, Writer's Club Press, offering online distribution of book via Amazon (com & co.uk), Barnes & Noble, Buy.com, Booksamillion.com, Walmart.com, Mediaplay.com and other online bookstores.

Quote
The quote is a set up fee of £700 plus royalties per sale or discounts to author.

Their print-on-demand service includes:
- DESIGN: bespoke design or development of your ideas – all included in the price
- EDITING: unlimited; advises on all aspects of the book including title, chapter titles, prelims, marketability etc
- PROOF-READING: All-inclusive in the price
- PRODUCTION & PRINTING: £700 set up
- SHORT PRINT RUN AVAILABILITY? tbc
- REGISTRATIONS: they register the book with Bowker and obtain the ISBN in America, under the imprint Writer's Club Press or iUniverse. Legal deposits are up to the author to do. Authors must buy their books at discount, see below.
- BOOK PRICE: The US selling price is determined in the US and this usually translates quite well into the UK. A 62,000 word book should therefore be comfortably under £10.
- FREE COPIES: 5 paperbacks within £700 set up fee; and 1 hardback if that option is chosen.
- ADDITIONAL COPY COST: see below
- ROYALTIES: 20% per book
- UK DISTRIBUTION: on Diadem website
- US DISTRIBUTION: via Bowker, their database makes your book available to order via online retailers such as B&N, Amazon.com and 25,000 booksellers worldwide. Online searches include key-words that are supplied online to the bookstores.
- MARKETING: services available additionally - toolkit to create own press release, sell sheet, event sign, postcards, bookmark,

- ADDITIONAL SERVICES AVAILABLE:
  - Provide both e-book and paperback
  - A hard-cover edition with own ISBN for £199

Author discounts:

Authors receive a 45% discount on the first order of at least 30 books or more. After that, the range is 20%-65% as per the following random examples:

1-9 books	= 20% discount
100-249	= 45%
500-999	= 55%
1000-1999	= 60%
2000+	= 65%

Bookstore discounts

Bookstores are offered discounts depending on the quantity ordered ie. 1-249 books, they get 25% or 50% discount if they order 1000 or more books. They can order directly from the publisher or via a wholesaler depending on their policies.

Summary

I am sure Diadem Books will provide a top quality, attentive service with a good jacket design, and I like the idea of a hard-cover edition with own ISBN. This is a nice touch.
The distribution channels certainly make a book available to order online on a global scale, but I'm unclear about the bookstores who buy firm at 25% discount as most of them demand a minimum of 35% (45% for most chains). The maths may still work out for the author depending on the book price, particularly as the upfront investment is low.

Lulu: www.lulu.com
No set-up fees. No minimum order. No catch.

Website

Lulu lets you publish a real book and sell it to the world. With POD, you are in control of the rights, the design, the price. You create an account, upload your work (books, calendars, songs), set up your royalty, publish and promote.

Quote

Lulu.com do not make a charge for uploading your book onto their site. They have a process which, correctly followed, will produce a virtual book that is ready to be printed on demand. Either 6x9" or 8.5x11" book perfect bound:

Binding fee	$4.53
B/W per page	$0.02
Colour per page	$0.15

Lulu's print-on-demand service includes:

- DESIGN: upload a finished design (front and back cover) as a JPG format fitted to the trim size. Lulu also offers a free gallery of standard covers to choose from
- EDITING: upload a finished PDF or formatted Word document. You will be able to view and print the PDF prior to your publication approval.
- PROOF-READING: none
- PRODUCTION & PRINTING: royalties only; no charges
- SHORT PRINT RUN AVAILABILITY? Only if you order through the site (see discounts)
- REGISTRATIONS: Once you have created a book on your project page, you can add/purchase an ISBN. This can be done at any point, even after you have published the book on Lulu.
- BOOK PRICE: as illustrated in above QUOTE section
- FREE COPIES: none
- ADDITIONAL COPY COST: $8.93 each / £6.00 each
- ROYALTIES: you set it
- UK DISTRIBUTION: Amazon UK distribution is available with the Global ISBN. Lulu are also actively working to establish a print partner in the UK so that titles purchased through the Lulu site are printed locally. In the meantime, free Supersaver shipping is available on international orders between $25 and $100.

- US DISTRIBUTION: ISBN assignment gets the book carried in almost all online book retailers.
- MARKETING: This may not be relevant, but there is an active community that develops and exchanges marketing advice and tips, as well as a free marketing kit that is somewhat helpful.
- ADDITIONAL SERVICES AVAILABLE: can publish calendars and music too, and there is a Marketplace so you can find a whole range of services that you might need to publish and promote.

Assessment

Lulu earn their money back by acting as the 'retailer' for books published through them, adding a percentage to your profit price.
ie. your book to the customer would cost:

$ tbc	production cost
$ 5.00	your mark-up
$ 1.25	Lulu mark-up

To sell your book anywhere other than via Lulu, you will need to purchase an ISBN with Global Distribution Service for $149.95. Lulu will then assign and register an ISBN on your book's behalf, add a barcode to the back of your book, and enter your book into the wholesale book catalogs from which the retailers draw their inventory. In order to do this, you will need to create a "retail price" for your book that takes into account the discount required by the resellers.

For my romantic fiction title averaging around 220 pages on 8.5 x 11" size perfect bound, it would cost:

Production cost	$8.93	ie.	£6.00 per book
My mark-up	$3.30		£2.00 to sell via the Lulu site
Lulu's mark-up	$1.00		£0.60
Total to buyer	**$10.26**		**£8.60**

I believe that the maximum that anyone will pay for my book is £6.99 as it is an average sized 'light' easy-read – bearing in mind that these genre of books sell in supermarkets for under a fiver more often than not. So £8.60 via the Lulu site is the outside edge of what someone might pay. However, I want to sell it on the main circuit via Amazon, Barnes & Noble, Borders, Waterstones etc. Therefore I have to set a retail price and work down from there to see what I would get left with after retailer discounts and POD charges.

If I sell through Amazon:

Retail price per book ($15.95 ie.)	£11.99
Amazon take 60%, leaving	£ 4.80
Production cost deductions	.- £6.00
Profit/loss to me, per book	**- £ 2.00**

The only way to make a profit would be via Amazon Marketplace, which you have to fulfil, and books on the Marketplace are invariably 50% less than the price they could sell at in the high street. Given that £11.99 is an excessive price for the average fiction title, the chances of an author making a profit look slim.

Remember to add on the one-off global distribution charge amortised over the first 300 books.

Summary

It is what it says it is – a site to upload your finished manuscript and publish your book on Lulu's website..

PlaneTree Publishing: www.planetree-publishing.com
Publishing Services.

Literature

A print-on-demand service with a non-exclusive contract which may be terminated at any time, leaving you free to sell foreign distribution and film rights

Quote

To obtain quote, you need to use the price list and standard publishing agreement from the website; download and submit with your payment and manuscript. It is £350 per manuscript for formatting up to 90,000 words; POD; author receives one free copy.

Their print-on-demand service includes:

- DESIGN: choose a template or bespoke cover design for £200
- EDITING: no
- PROOF-READING: no
- PRODUCTION & PRINTING: £350 set up
- SHORT PRINT RUN AVAILABILITY? See additional copy cost
- REGISTRATIONS: yes, under Planetree ISBNs; supply to legal deposit under the £350 comprehensive package.
- SELLING PRICE: author decides
- FREE COPIES: 5 free under the £350 comprehensive package.
- ADDITIONAL COPY COST:
  - 33.3% off list price for 10-49 copies
  - 50% off list price for 50 or more copies
- ROYALTIES: 10% of net returns
- UK DISTRIBUTION: on Planetree website and all details are submitted to Nielsen bookdata, Gardners and Amazon.
- MARKETING: support package available additionally
- ADDITIONAL SERVICES AVAILABLE: List of additional services including marketing, additional author corrections after submission, editorial and proof reading service, US registrations, CD Rom creation and translation to other languages.

Summary

They offer sound advice as to how to submit the manuscript and you can choose a book jacket from a wide range of templates. It is probably a good, reasonably-priced service for a book with low-marketability.

Publish and be damned: www.pabd.com
Publish and sell your book in four easy steps.

Literature

The website provides authors with a series of automated tools that you can use to self-publish your own book. This is called independent publishing.

Quote

It is free to use tools to design (from a template), publish and sell your book on your own personal online bookstore. You set your own selling price, making royalties a thing of the past. The only charge is that you buy a minimum of 25 copies of the finished book

PABD print-on-demand service includes:

- DESIGN: £35 per hour
- EDITING: need to see manuscript to quote
- PROOF-READING: £175 p/40,000 words; £4 p/1000 words thereafter
- PRODUCTION & PRINTING: £350 set up
- SHORT & LONG PRINT RUN AVAILABILITY? Yes; can move to short and long print runs; quote as required
- REGISTRATIONS: yes - PABD provide an ISBN number which is registered to yourself as the publisher; you can provide your own logo. They send legal deposit books. If you buy Publishing Plus package (£198.50) book goes onto Amazon.com as well.
- BOOK PRICE: author sets own price; they recommend authors set a personal selling price and book trade price to take into account book trade discounts.
- FREE COPIES: none; free service with only condition being you buy 25 copies of the book.
- ADDITIONAL COPY COST:
    - one off copies at print price (ie. 200 page book is £6.59 per copy); discounts for volume.
    - If you buy the Publishing Plus package, you buy one off copies at £4.70.
- ROYALTIES: 100% of net returns
- UK DISTRIBUTION: online presence and computer database ordering; Amazon.co.uk take 35% and Amazon.com take 30%
- MARKETING: Marketing handbook downloadable; they advise that this is section of the website attracts the most regular updates.

- ADDITIONAL SERVICES AVAILABLE:
  - Exclusive picture library
  - Custom designed covers
  - Full colour picture books
  - Editing and proofreading services
  - Run competitions

Summary

Very 'next-generation' approach to publishing; brave; doesn't adhere to any of the traditional avenues. The types of books on the site are very much what I would expect to find – gritty, self-expression and utterly contemporary. The site is very much a community, with competitions, interviews and lots of advice.

PABD comment:

There are huge opportunities in publishing today for self-publishing authors, and we think it is great that this book is putting a stake in the ground, with a view to helping businesses to regulate and authors to understand what is possible and not possible.

We are building an online community for self-publishing authors in order to offer help and advice. We have great links with other fantastic online writing communities, which are all listed on our website.

Publish Britannica: www.publishbritannica.com
Publishes books in the best tradition of old-fashioned quality publishing. Print-on-demand offer.

Their website advises that they charge no fees to the author, but only offer a contract if they believe book has market potential. They are interested in all genres of manuscript

To obtain a contract, email with information about manuscript and why you believe it is marketable; include a brief biography, your email address and SAE. There is one standard package for new authors and the decision may take up to several months. Royalties to author 8% on first 2000 copies; 10% on next 8,000 copies; 12.5% on copies over 10,000.

The contract is for a <u>seven</u> year duration.

- DESIGN: will either do cover design or take on board author's suggestions/designs
- EDITING: After the contract is signed, the author gets one last chance to make changes then it goes straight to page-proofs; no changes are possible except very minor corrections.
- PROOF-READING: no
- PRODUCTION & PRINTING: yes; free of charge
- ROYALTIES: to author are:
    - 8% on first 2000 copies;
    - 10% on next 8,000 copies;
    - 12.5% on copies over 10,000.
- REGISTRATIONS: yes
- DISTRIBUTION: online distribution worldwide
- MARKETING: Helpful hints about how to do it yourself
- ADDITIONAL SERVICES AVAILABLE: none mentioned

Summary

I contacted them with a list of questions, but was just re-directed to the website and advised that I could discuss the questions with an editor if my book was selected for publication. I don't know why the big secret; most authors would like to have answers *before* signing a contract for 7 years.

The lengthy contract period raises some questions too. A seven year contract with an 8-12.5% royalty rate, for print-on-demand and online distribution only?

Questions to Publish Britannia:

- What is your background expertise in publishing, and/or what authors/titles have you published that I might have heard of?
- Do you give advice on content and copy edit, including advice on title, back jacket text, author biography, chapter titles and general preliminary text?
- Do you offer any proof-reading?
- Is the book registered under your imprint, or do I set one up?
- Do I set the price of the book?
- It is print-on-demand, isn't it? Do I get any books free? How much do I have to pay for further copies?
- Can I sell it direct to the bookshops myself and keep 100% royalties?
- Can you advise me on wholesaling and/or distributing, other than online distribution?
- What do you mean about registering the book with the UK Copyright Centre?
- The 7 year contract bit… does this mean I cannot sell it myself, or sell any rights to other countries or whatever?

Trafford Publishing UK Ltd: www.trafford.com
On-Demand Publishing Service

Literature

Their website and literature announce that they were the first to offer on-demand publishing services that democratised the publishing process. Trafford is a Canadian company, now set up in England. The complete process can happen within 6 weeks. It is worth knowing that the books are printed in Canada and shipped to the UK; however; author only pays shipping from the UK address in Oxford.

Quote

To obtain your quote, send a hard-copy of your manuscript with a photocopy of a book's page to show how you want it to look; a sketch of the cover plus any artwork; meta-data information and the contract, witnessed by friend or neighbour. Chart of print cost and retail pricing ie. on a 260page paperback book, cover price is recommended to be £11.28; for 100 copies the per unit price is £4.24; and 500 copies the per unit price is £3.97.

Choose from one of six packages:

NB. Difference between Classic and Plus is that for Classic you do inside page layout yourself.

Package	Price	Free books	Extras
Legacy Classic	£499	10	
Legacy Plus	£849	10	
Entrepreneur Classic	£749	30	100 postcards
Entrepreneur Plus	£1099	30	100 postcards
Best Seller Classic	£999	50	10 posters 300 bookmarks 100 postcards
Bestseller Plus	£1349	50	10 posters 300 bookmarks 100 postcards

Their print-on-demand service includes:

- DESIGN: author submits layout; they artwork & proof
- EDITING: optional depending on service
- PROOF-READING: no, but have an online list of proof-readers, and advise that some authors approach university students
- PRODUCTION & PRINTING: POD; if I order 300, they are shipped to me at book print cost + shipping charges.
- SHORT PRINT RUN AVAILABILITY? On request
- REGISTRATIONS: provided with an ISBN, barcode and library catalogued in Canada. Books go under the Trafford imprint unless you want to create your own logo.
- BOOK PRICE: book price on Trafford website and other online listings is usually 2.5x the book print cost.
- FREE COPIES: see service level
- ADDITIONAL COPY COST: printing; see table of costs
- ROYALTIES: 60% of retail price less print cost & trade discounts.
- UK/US DISTRIBUTION: Online distribution via computer databases, depending on package chosen
- MARKETING: On Bestseller packages, you get your webpage promoted to internet search engines, your book's launch advised to industry and media contacts, promotional collateral and the opportunity to share ad space in the NY Times.

Example calculation

My book price is advised as being £11.28 based on page count. NB. This is not a price point therefore calculations based on £10.99:

Retail price	£10.99
less Amazon discount of	60%
Return to author	£4.39
Less print cost of	£4.51 (as per published table)
LOSS per book	**£0.11 pence per book**

Summary

Seems to be a very solid service, but the book price of £10.99 is still an unfeasibly high price for a romantic fiction. As my editor pointed out, Mills & Boon titles retail for around £4.99; contemporary chick-lit for £6.99. Also, delivery times from Canada may push you out of the market.

Writers Services : www.writersservices.com

The Website for writers – over 1200 pages of information

Website

The website advises that the Writers Printshop provides a design, production and distribution service using Print-on-demand technology. They help you get your book printed cost-effectively, so that you can focus on the demand, before and after publication.

Quotes are self-calculated from the website.

Their print-on-demand service includes:

- DESIGN: see section on website
- EDITING: see section on website
- PROOF-READING: see section on website
- JACKET TEXT: authors write it, but Writers Services review it
- PRODUCTION & PRINTING: POD
- SHORT PRINT RUN AVAILABILITY? tbc
- REGISTRATIONS: authors provide their own imprint name and logo; Writers Services offer an ISBN number from their allocation.
- PRICE OF BOOK: Author sets it.
- FREE COPIES: no
- ADDITIONAL COPY COST: reprinting
- ROYALTIES: Authors manage the full distribution and sales process, therefore own 100% of net receipts. As with most POD, based on a 200 page book retailing at £6.99, booksellers would take all the profit, leaving the author with only a few pennies.
- UK DISTRIBUTION: no
- MARKETING: fill out the marketing information form; fiction is very hard to sell; lifestyle, football and business books sell far better.
- ADDITIONAL SERVICES AVAILABLE: see the website

Summary

A comprehensive site with loads of information if you hunt around.

Writers Services comment

Biggest cynicism about the industry is when people claim to "publish your book for free" as nothing in life is free. They charge a high unit price whilst you do all the work; they do not feed information into the Bookdata system properly nor undertake the Legal Deposit obligation.

Writersworld : www.writersworld.co.uk
THE book production company; Print-on-demand offer

Website

A book publisher based in the United Kingdom and Spain that publishes worldwide in English and Spanish; specialises in print-on-demand and book reprints.

Quote

There are two template service packages available. The Enhanced Package costs £1,798 and you receive the following services:

Their print-on-demand service includes:

- DESIGN: bespoke cover design
- EDITING & PROOF-READING: yes
- PRODUCTION & PRINTING: Setting up for the writer and independent account with the printer wherein the PDF files for the cover and content will be loaded. The writer's address and all relevant financial details entered along with that of the Legal Deposit Agencies. Writer has own Username and Password and at any time can change account details and order as many copies of his or her book they wish at the actual cost the printer charges.
- REGISTRATIONS: Author owns all rights to the book Writersworld supplies ISBN and barcode and sends out the books for legal deposit.
- PRICE OF BOOK: set by author
- FREE COPIES: none mentioned
- ADDITIONAL COPY COST: Author buys the books direct from the printer at cost (1p p/ page and 70p for the cover).
- ROYALTIES: Author keeps 100% of the royalties ie. the difference between retail price less book retailer's commission and print cost.
- UK/US DISTRIBUTION: Books are listed on online databases to all UK & US wholesalers/ distributors and will be available to order via all internet bookshops - Amazon, B&N, Bol, Waterstones, WHS, Ottakars, Hammicks, Blackwell's, Methven etc. All US orders are printed and distributed there.
- MARKETING: Promotion to the trade via monthly Ingram's Advance notification service, the Amazon "Search Inside Book " programme and Googleprint to allow prospective buyers to run a keyword search across Google that will pick up the title and text.

Monthly classified ads will be run in The Bookseller, announcing Writersworld new titles; and a Press Release package will be available as an additional option.

- ADDITIONAL SERVICES AVAILABLE:
  - Translation and publication into Spanish.
  - Discounts to bona fide community service projects, charities or school year books.
  - Website optimization and search engine submission service for authors who have Websites.
  - Discounts available for more than one book submitted.

Summary

The offer seems very solid, and the Spanish element could prove to be a great exploitable opportunity – not only for Spain and South American countries, but also for the Spanish-speaking communities of America.

SUMMARY

The publishing and book-selling world is undeniably in a great state of change, and this is the reason why so many opportunities exist to unknown authors today. Traditional publishing and bookselling methods are blending with new technologies and new routes to market.

There is most marked difference between the English approach and US approach. American self-publishing companies coming over here are not hampered by the cautions and caveats that dominate the promises made by English companies. Whilst UK companies dance delicately around the issue of whether they are vanity or not, whether producing a book guarantees selling a book etc, the American's just hoe in, announcing 22,000 new titles produced, vast websites of books, shouting out about the 1% that achieved anything.

It is interesting to compare the US one-size-fits-all approach that the American businesses are offering with the cottage industry 'nurturing' offer that defines the existing UK market. Most of the English websites and literature lack the marketing glitz and promises of the US self-publishers, but there is a passion and individualism to them that an author's book deserves. It will be interesting to see how the imported, online based offers survive in the British market, and how they have to mould to fit our fussier needs!

The evaluation presents a scene of charming chaos.

It is commonplace in an emerging industry for this degree of haphazard, non-regulation to be evident as cottage industry blends with new professional business launches and corporate off-shoots.

There is plenty of opportunity both for the aspiring author and the publisher offering the services.

The motives for the majority of the self-publishing companies, the editors and the printers I interviewed largely revolved around the desire to offer authors a genuine route to market. They despair of the closed shop attitudes of the past, and work hard at trying to eradicate the residual negative attitudes of independent authoring and publishing. This is not just a money-making exercise to lighten authors of their money, but a genuine desire to make a difference. They are all keen to see regulation in the self-publishing services business that will best inform the author as well as level the playing field for them. They seek clarity and transparency from their competition; they want honesty in a category tarnished with a 'dishonest' reputation. This can only be achieved when everyone is clear and transparent about what the author gets, and doesn't get – and delivers according to their promises. In the meantime, many companies advise they end up over-delivering in order to reiterate their good intentions and quality of service.

You get what you pay for

It was an enormous task to try to standardise the different services offered and gain adequate information to compare like-with-like – particularly as some of the bigger web-based companies took a while to respond. The most interesting fact is that, on price, the industry is fairly well self-regulated.

Printing an averagely written, unedited book and listing it on a computer database is not publishing.

The strongest sentiment shared by many publishers and self-publishers is the fact that publishing and printing are two separate activities entirely, and authors should not get confused, as this will undoubtedly lead to failure. Missing out on the vital processes of editing, typesetting and design will only result in the printing of a poor quality book which won't ultimately sell. Many of the full services company shared the reservation that online publishing encourages authors to not recognise and implement these important processes – but instead get dazzled with how cheaply they can get their book from manuscript to print.

PART VI

GETTING THE MOST FROM A SELF-PUBLISHING SERVICES COMPANY

The purpose of this chapter is to interpret the evaluation. The lack of standardisation can be bewildering for the first-time author; therefore, in this chapter, we look at what is offered and what an author should expect.

ADVICE AND GUIDANCE

COMMON CONFUSIONS AND CAVEATS

WHO ARE THE COWBOYS

CHOOSING YOUR ROUTE TO PUBLICATION

QUESTIONS TO ASK CHECKLIST

TIMELINE TO PUBLICATION

ADVICE AND GUIDANCE

Critical assessment

Most self-publishing companies do not offer critical assessment, but this is a tricky area. Self-publishing companies are damned if they do, and damned if they don't. If they do, they are criticised for charging money to falsely praise a manuscript in order to secure the contract; if they don't, they are criticised for just publishing anything.

Those that undertake paid-for assessments advise that they use it to inform the contract and charges. In the absence of this, authors should seek independent editorial opinion.

The argument for an independent edit/critique

- What is it that makes a text successful? Is it just the compelling telling of a story? Is it because of the intrigue of the story itself? Is it because you empathise with the main character? Does it shows you a new perspective? There are many reasons and levels on which a story works, and it is very difficult for a new author really to assess if they have achieved what they set out to achieve.
- Have you said what you wanted to say? Are your characters plausible and well-drawn?
- There are literary standards and structures because they have been proven to work over millions of text. We all laugh about the American thriller film standards – one handsome hero, one evil person, some battles, some sex and some comedy/sadness/moralising etc. We laugh, but we still go to see the films. They work.
- Television sit-coms and productions are invariably written by a team of writers – and they are good. The dialogue is sharp and the storyline is thorough and realistic. If you

want to ensure your text is really sharp, get at least one other person to look at it. Maybe a whole team?

- If you are approaching the literary agents and mainstream publishers, then your work has to be really competitive and polished. Therefore, the investment is worth it.
- If you are going down the self-publishing route, you are about to spend a lot of money, time and effort. You need to ensure at the outset it is worth it.

The argument against an independent edit/critique

The majority of editors will judge according to age-old traditions and standards. If you are trying something new or different, or you have a challenging subject matter then you might come up against reservations or criticism. GP Taylor had his work edited by an online editor, who commented that it wasn't good and wouldn't sell, although largely based on subject-matter rather than writing style. Fortunately, Graham chose to ignore these criticisms and went on to get a mainstream deal with Faber & Faber and sell 70,000 books in the initial launch phase.

**If you are going to ignore advice,
at least know what advice you are ignoring**

Editing

The term *editing* is a catch-all for quite a wide description, and any authors buying into an editing service will need to be clear about what they are paying for. A content edit is more comprehensive than a copyedit. Most companies do not offer editing as an integral part of the package – some offer it as an optional extra and the other half do not offer it at all. Yet the majority of authors need editing.

Content edit

A content edit is when the editor comments on the overall viability of a story, its structure and pace, character development, continuity and consistency.

Copy-editing

A copy edit is when the editor corrects spellings, grammar and punctuation. If you are using a US-based company, double check what spell-checker they are using. You do not want to have a UK title with American spellings, words and grammar.

UK books must use
British language & grammar

Proof-reading

Firstly, *proof-reading* and *proofing* are two totally different items. Proof-reading is the letter by letter, word by word, typos, spelling, grammar and punctuation final read-through. It is the last point at which text changes can be made before it goes to the printer. It is done on a typeset, print-ready document. Last minute corrections are made before the work goes to the printer.

The printer will then *proof* the file which means they create a *printed proof* of the book. This is designed to check that the digital file has been correctly read and printed; that no pages are missing; that overall page layout and margins are accurate; it is positioned straight on the page; that the headers or footers aren't too close to the page edge; that there is no show-through. If you make any text changes at this point, you have to go back a step, alter and re-submit to the printer who will charge again to make a second print-proof. Once the print-proof has been signed off by the author/publisher, it then goes to the full print run. Don't get confused, as this could be an expensive confusion.

Most of the self-publishing services companies do not offer a proof-reading service, as this is costly (£15-30 per hour) and it just prices them out of the competition. Some of them offer it as an additional extra. But most assume that this is a task that you, as the author, will choose to do. After all, you have to sign it off or live with any errors.

Double check with them before you sign any agreements or contracts as to what any references to proofing actually include.

Proofing and proof-reading are two separate activities

Jacket cover design

Some of the companies offer a comprehensive jacket design service, and you can get a very good idea of whether you like their style of design by looking at their literature/website. They are completely open to you coming along with your own ideas, and will advise you based on their knowledge of the industry and expertise in design. The wise author takes this on board.

Most of the companies offer an artwork service ie. bring along your ideas and any photographs or illustrations, and they will design around it. This isn't necessarily a bad thing, but it is difficult to ascertain their degree of expertise both in graphic design for a book jacket and knowledge of the book market. You can really only judge it by looking at their other titles and seeing what they produce for you.

I am sure that for most of these companies, they will do you a different cover included within the price, if you really don't like what they have done. But I doubt they will do this too many times before they have to make a charge and will ask you to re-define your brief.

Some of the companies, particularly the online POD companies, only offer a template design service or expect you to supply your own artwork. For some people this is obviously fine, but for the majority it means you will have paid someone independently (or cashed in a huge favour with a friend) to get a piece of jacket design.

Having spent 12 years of my life working in design agencies on global brands, I know how sensitive design is and the massive role it plays in purchase decisions. Research from BML, as detailed earlier in the book, also demonstrates what a major influence the book jacket has on reader's decisions. One interesting observation is that whilst the text didn't change as the self-published author sold to a mainstream publisher, the cover did. Pretty much every time. That might simply be the publisher's desire to put their own stamp on a book, but I doubt it. Each time the cover changed, it invariably changed to something better. The only exception that I have seen was George Courtauld's *Pocket Book of Patriotism*. The cover design remained fairly true to the cover he launched as a self-published author. Well done him!

Have the book jacket professionally designed

Jacket text copywriting

Few self-publishing companies mention who writes this, with the exception of one or two companies. I suspect for the majority, the author has to write it and the only advice I have in this circumstance is to go and get a book that teaches you the art of copywriting. You don't need me repeat what an important part of the reader's decision-making process it is.

You need to have a real economy with words, and create short, punchy, impactful sentences that tell the reader (i) what the book is about (ii) why they should read it (iii) that it is aimed at them (iv) how it will leave them feeling – all written in a style that appeals and conveys the tone of the story. All this in 100 words.

I send my back text off to my editor, written in 200 words with a sample of the style ie. 2-3 chapters, with the brief to get it down to 100 or less… all the more space for reviews!

Cover text must be carefully crafted and considered

Production values

With so many averagely-produced self-published titles, it is important to get your head above the crowd by producing a title that looks exactly like a mainstream printed book. Most of the companies stress the quality of their work in this area, and the only real way to judge is to ask them for a random sample of titles and check it for yourself – bearing in mind that they will send you the best.

If you don't like the page layout or you spot loads of typos, then they are not the company to do business with.

Formats

Some of the UK companies recommended non-standard formats for the category I was writing, which surprised me. Fiction is generally 129x198mm (also known as B format), whereas self-help and business books tend to be larger ie. up to 234x156mm (also known as Royal Octavo).

Authors using a US company should check what format the book is being created as 5½ x 8 inches is standard in the US, but this is a non-standard UK format.

Printing a book is a different activity from publishing a book

Printing

This is central to the service that all the self-publishing service companies run. It is the part of the process that most of their offers revolve around, and the self-publishing author would be wise to make this a primary decision factor (see Choosing a Route on page 273).

The decision should be based on all the pros and cons as listed in the earlier sections (POD and short print run). To add to this, I would suggest that, if you are looking for a very global, international market, then POD may be the better offer if you can control the selling price. If you are looking to launch into a local or regional market, then short print run has the edge. Whichever one you choose, you will lose a lot of margin to the middle-man. At least in a local market, you can sell direct, which means you make a lot more per book. And whatever you do, don't do print-on-demand if you are selling via bookshops. You will be left with no profit – maybe you'll even end up paying for the honour of someone buying your book.

Determine the ideal print method according to your market

Managing the print

Another question to consider is at what point should you move from digital printing short print runs and move to a litho-printed long print run. Experts in the industry advise that once you are running more than 300 copies at once, you should go straight to a long print run using a litho printer.

This raises another question. Should you just go straight to a long print run on the very first print? Personally I don't recommend it, but opt for a run of 50-100 digitally printed copies on a short print run. I then work like crazy to get reviews and endorsements to incorporate onto the cover, then go for a longer print run of 1000. This is a healthy challenge – you have got them at a decent cost per unit and now you just have to sell them. The longer they sit in your house, they are worth nothing.

Reprinting

Only two of the companies offered a reprinting service inclusive within the initial price. The Book Guild who quoted £8,800 for a full service, hard-back edition and Pen Press, who quoted £3,250 for a full service, paperback edition. Both still offer the author a sizeable 35% of monies returned. Bearing in mind that printing is the single most expensive item you will pay for in self-publishing, I found this a motivating factor. Another method of reprinting is Ashridge's service – he offers to fund the reprint, giving authors 7.5% royalties on sales. For all the other companies, I would have had to plough back all of my profits to get another print run.

And how risky is it to get another print run? Oftentimes for a new author, the market is saturated after the initial launch phase or within the first year – I am talking specifically about biographies and fictional titles. Self-help, business and religious books tend to have a longer selling period and many more incremental markets that you can continue approaching and selling to. For biographies and fictional titles, there are fewer locatable market groups or communities, and you have to do a more 'scatter-gun' approach.

Plan your print strategy at the outset

Registrations

When you use UK-based companies to produce your title, they are obviously registering your book with Nielsen Bookdata, with a UK price and an ISBN number that is registered to a UK-based company name.

It is also worth checking whether you get a say in what the summary book description is when your book is being registered to Nielsen, because the quality of information is critical. It must accurately reflect the nature of the book.

Good information in, good information out. It is the difference between your book being found, and not.

Free copies and buying additional copies

The number of free copies varied from none to fifty, but upon closer inspection, this figure was closely tied up with how much you had paid for the service. PABD don't charge for their service at all, and therefore don't offer any free copies; Authors Online charge £1,450 for their POD service for which you get 20 free books.

If you are paying for a print run, then all the copies should technically be yours depending on the ongoing services. If the publishing company manage the whole 'post-production' elements ie. distribution, fulfilment, warehousing, stock management, royalties and invoicing, then this must be paid for, usually in royalties.

The Book Guild and Pen Press plough their part of the royalty percentage from the sale of your book back into the next print run. This rarely fully funds the next print run, but it is a service that authors have found invaluable as it limits their own risk.

Be clear about what you are getting at the outset of the agreement

Royalties

It is commonplace for companies to exchange royalties for any post-production services ie. promoting books to trade, fulfilling orders, stock management and warehousing, royalties, sale/returns and invoicing. Given that experienced self-publishers say this is the most tedious part of self-publishing, the savvy self-publisher will gladly hand this over for a reasonable share of royalties.

Another critical area to understand is the sheer length of time before royalties become a financial 'hard-cash' reality. It can take up to six months after print and distribution before you may see the first penny; often more like a year. This means you are bank-rolling the cost of editing, design, production and printing for a long time, so it is important that authors do not see this investment as 'borrowing some money for a short while'.

Publishing means bank-rolling a print run for at least a year

What is a reasonable royalty rate?

The average seems to be the Author giving the Publisher 10-15% of net receipts; this seems reasonable for the company that doesn't include reprinting within their service.

For companies that pay for ongoing print runs, the Author should expect to give the Publisher around 65% of net receipts which is ploughed back in to reprinting and maintaining promotion of the title to the trade. The author still gets 35%, but without the expense of bank-rolling the print and the cost of fulfilment.

Equally, authors can choose to retain 100% of the royalties by taking the full delivery of the books and managing the sales end of the process themselves.

What are net receipts?

"Net receipts" is the standard industry term for the money that comes back to the publisher once the many middlemen have taken their piece of the pie and the reader has had the title heavily discounted in order to sell it. It is this figure which is divided up between the author and publisher in line with contractual royalty percentages.

An example calculation: mainstream published books

Let's assume that you, the author, are getting 8% of net

Book price:	£7.99
Average bookseller discount:	50%
Net receipts back to publisher:	£3.99
Publisher takes 92%	£3.67
Author receives 8% net	£0.32

You, the author, get 32p per book sold. If 1000 books are printed AND sold, you get £320. Wahey! Bring on the champagne. You need to sell 10,000 to get £3,200 which is the average after-tax pay for a salaried person – in two months.

This is why it is so difficult to make a living out of writing. Hopefully the Rights department are selling translation rights, publishing, tv and broadcasting rights around the world to bump the numbers up a bit.

Comparison calculation: a self-published title

Production of book	(not included in calculation)
Book price:	£7.99
Sell 200 via wholesaler @ 45%	+ £878.90
Sell 500 via a bookseller @ 35%	+ £2,597
Sell 100 via Amazon @ 60%	+ £310.00
Sell 200 privately @ 100%	+ £1,598
Author receives 100% net	£5,393

However... this firstly assumes that you HAVE sold all 1000 books, which is a difficult task in itself. Then you have to deduct all your expenses such as travel, parking, postage & packing, banner advertisements. Given that many of the books will have been fulfilled incrementally, this is not going to be cheap. **Deduct £2,000** for all these expenses (at least).

You've still made a fair whack, but it has taken all your time over several months whereas for the mainstream contract you could actually have been earning money elsewhere whilst someone tried to sell the book for you. And then you have to plough that back into reprint – and this doesn't include your initial investment of c. £2,000 which you are going to write off until such time as you are turning a steady profit.

POD - for each book the POD Publishers sells

Production of book (not included in calculation)	
Book retails at	£7.99
Printer takes 80% book price	- £6.00
Deducts all shipping / taxes	- £1.00
Author receives per book	**+ £1.00**

Therefore, if I have 1000 books printed in total, and half are sold via the POD publisher's website, 250 via my book-signing events and 250 via Amazon Marketplace, I get a total of £750. Given that my original production costs were £700, I am £50 up on the deal.

Confusing percentage return on RRP with net receipts can be an expensive mistake

Distribution

"Available via all good bookshops..."

Most of the companies we looked at advise that your book will be for sale via all the big book chains and retail outlets - Barnes & Noble, Borders, Waterstones, Tesco's etc. And this is true.

However, this is an "easy to misunderstand" phrase. When self-publishing and POD companies say that your book will be available via all major booksellers, they mean exactly that – VIA. It means that your book is registered to Nielsen Bookscan or Bowker Books in Print, which is a computer database that booksellers use to update their own databases. So when a friend of yours goes to "Books Are Us" and requests your book, it can be found on the database either by Author Name, Book Title or ISBN number (the latter being the most reliable and robust method of finding a low-selling or new title).

To get your book physically distributed through all the book chains in today's saturated market is nigh on impossible, and therefore it is no longer reasonable for authors to expect to have physical distribution on a national scale. When established authors are having their books returned after 4 months of a non-sale, the unestablished authors really don't stand a chance. You need to work hard at drumming up your audience, establishing your reputation as an author and proving yourself before you have earned a place in national distribution. If you get it without years of hard work, then well done you! Celebrate hard!

Establish your reputation
before you expect to have national distribution

Online distribution

The majority of companies offer online "distribution". This is not distribution in the traditional sense of the word.

Distributors are people who stock your book, include it in sales catalogues, have sales reps who promote your title to certain channels, fulfil actual sales and endeavour to get physical copies of your book into as many retail outlets as possible.

Online distribution is similar in that they hold a 'virtual stock' of your book which is printed as soon as it is demanded and paid for; they include jacket image and text on their site (ie. their catalogue) and they fulfil actual sales. But they do not actively promote your title and do not seek to get hardcopy stock in other retail outlets.

Technology doesn't make the middle-men go away; it just changes the middle-men

But you must ask yourself - who goes to the websites of self-publishers? Answer: other authors looking to self-publish, not buyers of books necessarily. In a recent conversation, a buyer at a major book store reiterated this belief, confirming that few people are interested in reading books that are promoted as self-published titles. However, people happily read self-published titles when they don't know they have been self-published. Ergo... it is critical that the self-published title looks and behaves exactly the same as a mainstream published title.

Any authors going down a 'virtual distribution' route must bear in mind that investment will need to be made in actively promoting their book to the target audience. Otherwise the book will just sit there as a description and an image for several years, unseen and unsold, lost in a sea of information...

Google is currently searching 8,000,000,000 pages of information (July 2005)

Widgets, or books, sold online with their own IP address which is actively and regularly re-promoted to the search engines with a good range of keywords, will stand a chance of the surfing buyer finding it – if they happen to be idly surfing and/or looking for your search words. Widgets, or books, sold online via a website that few people go to, probably won't sell. Remember, even if you have a web address, to host it, pay for content and manage it on a regular basis ie. update it with information about events, reviews, news information etc. People will return to websites if the information is (i) relevant and (ii) updated.

Budget for a website if relying on online distribution

Marketing

Very few self-publishing companies include marketing within their charges because it would make them uncompetitive price-wise. Marketing is a very time consuming task to do well. It is also an activity that should be undertaken BEFORE the book is launched and in my experience of book marketing, most authors do not realise what they need and how much they need it until long after the launch of their book – when it is far too late.

Information readily available in the market will provide authors with outlined lists of what they should be doing, but this rarely translates into authors doing it successfully. Part of the reason is that writing is, in itself, a very solitary experience and many writers like this solitude. They therefore find it difficult to press people to write about their book or request an interview or ask if they will host a book event. It's not in their nature.

Equally, many authors are so close to their work that they can't see the wood for the trees. I have so many authors telling me what their book is about, but what they choose to describe is not the motivating reason to read it.

Marketing is not a bolt-on
but a continual process through the life of a book

Further information in "What do I have to do to sell a book!"
In the meantime, contact me via my website:
www.indepublishing.com

Nice-to-have extras

Some of these were really good, and it would be great if an author could just pick and choose, irrespective of who they go with. Obviously the "nice-to-haves" won't influence your decision on who to proceed with at a top-level, but it may be the deciding factor between two narrowed-down choices. The strongest ones for me were the UK sites that tried to build communities (PABD), the offer of audio books (Amolibros) and the trade fair attendances (Book Surge, Pen Press, Book Guild).

- audio books (Amolibros)
- sale of paperback and other rights (Book Guild)
- website activity ie. Newsflash (on Matador site); communities (PABD site), latest books scroll (AuthorsOnline); webpage promoted to internet;
- marketing services (Pen Press, Book Guild); book promoted to industry & media (Trafford)
- alternative imprints (Pen Press)
- E-books (AuthorsOnline, Diadem)
- Banner ads (Booksurge)
- Log of all book sales, royalties checker (AuthorsOnline)
- Amazon Marketplace Managed (Booksurge)

- Independent reader's assessment (Pen Press)
- Trade Fair package (Booksurge)
- Hardback edition - recommended (Book Guild); additional version (Diadem)
- Calendars and music upload (Lulu)
- Translations (Planetree); to Spanish (Writersworld)
- CD rom creation (Planetree)
- Picture library (PABD)
- Online competitions (PABD)
- Certain community production discounts ie. church, school yearbooks (Writersworld)

COMMON CONFUSIONS AND CAVEATS

There are many myths about publishing, self-publishing and bookselling. Here are a handful and I have no doubt many more will begin to emerge from the woodwork:

- Book publishing should not be confused with book printing – the services involved in publishing run to far more than a print service
- Do not confuse creative control with editing control – the two are very different. Retain the creative control, but allow editors to make editing changes
- Don't confuse royalties of 35% of net receipts as 35% of RRP; a large chunk of middle-man margin has been deducted before your royalty is calculated
- Don't think that "Available through all good bookshops" means actual presence in all good bookshops. It just means it's on a database
- Remember the book trade works on sale or return; just because you've despatched 2000 books to a major chain, it doesn't mean they are sold. They are just 'holding' the books until they either pay for them or return them.
- The book trade works on long lead times; even if the books actually sell, you will be bank-rolling the cost of production for a long time. Don't borrow money to fund it.
- Mass production does not an expert make; it just makes a mass-market
- Watch out on POD pricing; if the price is too high then no-one will buy it except your mum and dad. Book prices are very sensitive for unknown authors.
- Book reviewers only review hard-back books – NOT. Book reviewers are discerning on subject-matter not format, as long as the book format FITS to category. It is true to say

that national newspaper book reviewers tend to review more literary (prize-winning), academic, philosophic or autobiographic books. The fact that these are frequently published in hardback can lead people to believe that book reviewers only review hardback books.

- Having a domain name registered does not give you online presence; you have to create your website, host, update, promote and monitor it
- If you have an awkward spelling to your name, change your name to avoid getting lost on modern-day computerised databases which rely on perfect spelling and punctuation.
- Don't change your name from Jane Smith to Jayne Smythe in order to look creative and interesting. No-one will find you. *I have, however, heard of some authors changing their name in order to sit next to a famous author in the same genre eg. John Pulton may end up next to Philip Pullman on the shelf.*

WHY WOULD YOU PUBLISH WITH A SELF-PUBLISHING SERVICES COMPANY?

There are a number of reasons why an author might choose to work with a company offering the full range of services:

- Because they have experience of the publishing industry, and you may have no knowledge of the industry at all.
- They work with tried and tested editors, proof-readers and printers.
- They have established distributor/wholesaler and bookseller accounts.
- They have to stand by the reputation of their logo on the spine of the book.
- They offer a guaranteed delivery of finished product to a pre-agreed figure within a set time-frame.
- If they are actively promoting themselves, then they are actively promoting you.

- You can benefit from their 'community' ie. talk to other authors, share advertising and promotions, participate in events etc.

WHY WOULD YOU NOT PUBLISH WITH A SELF-PUBLISHING SERVICES COMPANY?

Some authors simply prefer to do it their own way, and remain completely in control. Also, there is a degree of apprehension in the industry about who offers what, and on the next page we look at "Who are the Cowboys?"

WHO ARE THE "COWBOYS"?

In the past, there have been problems with "cowboys" who have set up as publishers, charged excessively for services they are not qualified to offer and not fulfilled against their own contracts. They were given the name "Vanity Publishers" – although in today's world they would probably be called "rogue traders".

Sadly, many of the people who were most affected by this were old people, who simply wanted to leave a legacy for family, or who were trying to make money to see them through their old age. A number of campaigners supported their cause, and helped put the rogues out of business and they continue to campaign to ensure new rogue traders don't enter the market.

The new millennium has brought with it a range of new technologies and global bookselling market-places that provide budding authors with far greater opportunities – opportunities that simply weren't around twenty years ago. Accessibility to self-expression dominates today.

Yesterday's messages warning authors about Vanity Publishers mingle with today's websites that boast of 22,000 self-published authors. The self-publishing author is confused and, in his confusion, he risks spending his time and money unwisely. Below are some of the confusing messages out in the media today, together with an explanation.

Vanity publishers praise your work

And so does a mainstream publisher or agent…

The question is who is the judge of what is good or not? On what basis are they praising the work? If you get an independent editor to judge it, then you are likely to get an honest appraisal. They may not be the right person, and you may seek a second opinion, but they will be objective and honest.

They claim an independent judge has reviewed it
As above, an independent judge probably has reviewed your work and the only question is whether they are skilled in this area – and evidence of previous work will confirm this. Some of the self-publishing houses offer reader's reports which (i) provide an honest assessment of the work, and (ii) enable them to quote more accurately for the services you will need ie. degree of editing, type of services required. There is arguably an honesty in companies wishing to evaluate the work before quoting on it.

They print your work regardless of quality
Correct. Many of the self-publishing businesses, particularly the POD companies, are absolutely crystal clear that the quality of the work you choose to publish is completely up to you. You upload your finished manuscript and they print it. Tens of thousands of people have published in precisely this way, and continue to do so.

This doesn't make it right, but equally it doesn't make it illegal. It just means that it is all the more critical for the author to approach any contract knowing exactly what he needs and what he is getting.

You know it's Vanity because they ask for payment
Self-publishing businesses ask for payment because they are offering a range of services which they author wishes to buy from them. The question is whether they provide a good, solid, quality range of services – all of which can be judged by the books they produce and their track record.

At the very least, the person who pays for a service can complain when they don't get it; unlike mainstream published authors who report feeling let-down by the subsequent service they received, but felt they didn't have a leg to stand on because it was a royalties-based agreement.

There are many similar parallels:

(i) Music recording studios charge musicians, bands and singers for recording their music/song onto CD so they can take it round to production companies.
(ii) Models, actors and actresses pay photographers to create a portfolio for them that they can send to casting agents in order to get work.

It is no different when a first-time author decides to convert his type-written manuscript into book form in order to try to sell it into shops, sell it direct to interested readers or even just send it to agents to read. The only difference is whether someone makes false promises.

Vanity publishers charge £8-12,000 for 15 copies and more at a reduced price

These are obviously ridiculous prices, as can be seen from the range of quotes demonstrated in the Evaluation section in this book. Whilst there is still a lot of vagueness and lack of clarity in the market, price is not one of them. The self-publishing author would be wise to compare prices and criteria mapped out in this book in order to know the standards in the industry.

Vanity titles tend to be badly produced

Some books are badly produced, this is true, and there is no excuse for this. Authors are well-advised to request samples or visit the company prior to signing the contract. Be thorough - discuss and agree on an actual shop-bought sample to act as your blue-print. If both you and the publisher counter-sign two copies of the sample book and have one each, then there's no room for doubt as to what is being produced at the end of the process. Then it is up to both parties to work towards this throughout.

Vanity titles are badly edited – or not edited at all

When an author pays for an edit, he should expect a good level of editing. Different editors will edit differently, and judge a story differently. But, aside from difference of opinion, an edited work should meet a certain standard.

Graham Taylor confirms that his work was not altered when it was sold to Faber & Faber; only the cover. Ditto with Peter Murray who had his book edited and produced by Pen Press Publishers; the book sold 12,000 copies in the first three months and Peter secured a 3-book deal. When *Mokee Joe is Coming!* was relaunched under the Hodder name, none of the text was altered by the Hodder editors.

Many self-published titles are unedited, and this is often where they let themselves down under close scrutiny. Even when you have a professional cover and presentation, poorly written text or poorly structured plot will let you down.

Remember: a good cover around a poor story merely delays the moment the reader feels disappointed or let-down, and the author should take responsibility for this. If in doubt, then seek independent advice.

With self-publishing you retain all your rights; with vanity publishing you don't

The current self-publishing market clearly shows that in all the instances evaluated, authors owned 100% of the copyright of the text and royalties from the books until such time as they chose to trade royalties in exchange for ongoing sales services. The author finds himself giving away percentage royalty in order to buy in additional services, but this is not (and should not be) copyright.

Vanity publishers only pay you a small royalty on sales
Not the case. In all cases examined, the author owns 100% of royalties until they choose to 'trade' percentage royalty for ongoing services.

Vanity publishers own all of the books
Again, not the case. Under the non-POD contracts, authors own the books. Under POD, the author has to buy each book printed.

You will be asked to grant the publisher exclusive licence to exploit the work
I haven't examined each company's contract and I'm not a lawyer, so I recommend that you check the contract over carefully. If in doubt, take it to a lawyer or another self-publishing company.

Vanity publishers have no incentive to sell
Vanity publishers didn't have an incentive to sell. They allegedly charged so much for the production of the book, printed only a handful of the contracted print run, with the promise to print more if there was a demand. Given that the books were so shoddily produced, they knew no-one would buy them, so didn't bother to promote them.

In this evaluation, I haven't seen evidence of a company that works in this way but apparently they once existed. Maybe they still do, but in this increasingly competitive field, they really won't survive very long. Today's author pays less up front and owns all the royalties until he commissions a self-publishing company to promote and sell the title.

In fact, today's self-publishing author is far better off, as the self-publishing companies are competing to produce better and better work that sells in shops and wins awards. They want to do as big a print run as possible to get a lower cost per unit, then sell as many as possible to achieve as high a profit as possible. Their incentive is the additional income.

Vanity companies print to order... up to an agreed figure
POD companies certainly do. The others prefer to do the highest print run possible in order to get the litho-quality and lower cost per unit. If an author is concerned about a company's intention to print the full run, then have a one month notice "get out" clause in the contract.
"Once the original agreement has been paid in full, the author can issue a one month notice to receive the full print run of books, less any copies sold or otherwise issued (legal deposit, review copies)."

Vanity titles are rarely stocked by shops and libraries
In today's market, there are many mainstream published titles that aren't stocked in bookshops and libraries. The FIRST question is whether they offer post production services, and how are you paying for this? If you enter into an agreement whereby you are exchanging royalties for them to sell your book, then the real question is whether the publisher has a route to bookshops. Do they get books in locally? Do some books go national? Do they promote to the trade in any way, and have library accounts either direct or via their distributor? Again, check the publisher's track record of where books are sold through. Do your homework and maybe even speak to a bookshop that has hosted an event for them.

The ISBN belongs to the vanity/subsidy publisher, not the author
There is a school of thought that if YOU put your own publisher name and logo on the book and register the ISBN, then it is self-publishing. If you get a company to do it for you, then it is vanity publishing.

The reality is that the first five numbers of an ISBN number are a unique publisher prefix. When registering as a publisher, you nominate where book orders are routed through. Therefore, if you wish to control the sales and fulfilment, you should use your own ISBN. If you wish the self-publishing company to manage the sales, stock control and fulfilment, then use their ISBN so orders are routed back to them.

If you allow the self-publishers to use their own ISBN numbers, check where the numbers are routing through. Most self-publishing companies offering Sales services will use one of the big established wholesalers ie. Gardners, Bertrams or THE; or the emerging mid-sized companies like Gazelle or Central.

An additional school of thought is that, in this very competitive environment, the publisher's logo actually stands for a mark of quality and reputation. The books they create have to meet a certain standard as they are staking their personal reputations against it, and in this the logo can symbolise a standard of work.

Mainstream publishers never advertise for authors

No, they don't. But neither do they produce a piece of literature that extols their wares, their mission and vision, what they do and their specialist interests etc which is a shame. It would be interesting.

Nowadays, all of the self-publishing and POD companies advertise for authors. It is a standard, and therefore not a way to judge if a company is intending to do a shoddy job for good money.

If your work is good, a reputable publisher will do it without payment

Not always. By their own admission, they miss some because of the high volume of material that comes in to them. But mainstream publishers are prepared to acknowledge this fact, and there is a growing trend to watch the self-published titles for any little gems that emerge.

DTP software is so good that authors can do it themselves

The inference that you can master typesetting, page layout and publishing skills overnight is simply misleading. Just because you have a piano, it doesn't mean you can play it. Page and text layout is not as straightforward as it seems. It is easy to end up with rivers of white space down a page, widows (single words) left hanging on a new page, uneven page lengths etc.

The caveat that self-published titles are shoddy doesn't just mean that the glue is bad and the pages fall out. It means the overall layout looks home-made and unprofessional; that the age-old art of print and page layout is fundamentally lacking.

Will these things matter in 20 years time when everyone is banging out abbreviated text online? Already phone texting is impacting on spellings, abbreviations and written colloquialisms - but for the time being, it still counts.

Be clear about your chances of earning any money back from your investment

Indeed be clear – the likelihood of turning a profit is low and the wise author will not spend any money that he cannot afford to lose. The reality is that you will make back money if you sell books – your focus has to remain on how to sell them.

In summary...

This is quite a catalogue of accusations, which ultimately are unhelpful. Many of the points are out of date and this confuses the authors. This evaluation is designed to help authors to assess a company using the right criteria. Ultimately, you want to judge a company by their authors and the titles they are producing.

A good company is as flexible as it is transparent

CHOOSING YOUR ROUTE TO PUBLICATION

The point of this book is to help authors to understand the self-publishing market well enough to help you identify which is the best route for you. Each author has a different starting point, a different need and different objective and only you know what you are looking for. The route that is right for you will depend on whether you understand the process adequately to do it completely on your own? Or maybe you have contacts in the business who are willing to help you? Do you know what you can capably do yourself and what tasks you need to buy in? Do you know where you can cut costs in order to invest in something else ie. marketing, further down the line?

If you are intending to adhere to the advice "Don't give up the day job" then you are likely to be looking for a full services company who will manage the whole process for you and all you have to do is sign off and approve.

However, if you are on a six-month sabbatical and trying to launch your first book, then throw yourself into it by doing as much as you possibly can. There will still be items that you should buy in, and this isn't just the print, but more of that further on.

Know what you can do and what you need to pay for

Before plunging headlong into publishing, it is advisable to really understand why you are doing it. Authors say that often, when they start writing, that they don't really know why they feel compelled to write it. Sometimes a person just feels moved or inspired to write.

However, once you start investing money in it, you need to know what you've created and why. What are you hoping to achieve?

If you are writing a family history, then you don't really need to get an expensive edit, proof-read, cover design and 100+ print run done. You can edit and proof-read it yourself and pay a company to typeset and print to a limited number of copies ie. 25, 50 etc. And you can buy these sort of services very cheaply from companies who will provide a very solid quality of work.

If you are writing a 500-page saga, then you really want to be looking for a longer print run ie. 1000+ in order to be left with any margin at all once you have started selling.

Understand your reason for publishing to determine your financial investment and publishing strategy

Choosing a self-publishing services company

If you decide that you would prefer to work with a company who can produce the book on your behalf, the next decision is which company to work with.

Each self-publishing services company offers something different, and they base their quotations on a different set of criteria. This makes it difficult to assess them, but hopefully this evaluation will help you to understand who is offering what, and what you should be looking for. The main parameters that the self-publishing author should be looking for are:

First level:
Does the company offer Print-on-demand (POD) or Short Print Run? This makes an immediate difference to the whole

structure, benefits and constraints to a company's service and this may have a huge bearing on how you reach your audience.

If your audience is the 70+ age group, then they are unlikely to find you online – so you won't want to publish with a company restricted to online selling. You would be better off doing a short print run and finding a wholesaler who sells directly into community centres, libraries and old people's homes.

If your book is very UK-centric, then it will be immaterial whether you have US-distribution as you won't pick up a huge audience there.

Equally, if you are producing some kind of educational or training manual, then e-publishing is rapidly proving to be the way forward with maybe a POD hard-copy available to order; and if it is relevant to both UK and US markets, then go for a company that promotes heavily online to the widest possible audience.

Start with your audience in order to inform your decision-making

Second level:

Are they a UK or US-based business, as the two markets are very different? The price points that can be held in UK are different from the US, and if they are a POD company who set the price point, you will find you just can't sell in the UK at that price point – or in many other markets like India and Asia which have a staggeringly low price-point.

Where is the business centre based? Find out if you are dealing with someone in the UK, paying in pounds and being printed within the UK. Lower phone bills are one small mitigating factor, but if you are not being printed in the UK then you will be paying shipping costs from the US. If paying in dollars, then, as a UK resident, you may get benefits with the exchange rate, although this won't always be the case.

Third level:
What services do they offer? The range of criteria the services are mapped against depends on whether they offer POD or SPR.

Final level:
You may get down to the end of evaluating the services and be left with 2 or 3 that seem positive. At this point you should:

1. go and meet with them, see their current titles, chat to them about your needs
2. have a look at the nice-to-haves. Sometimes these might add an additional value to your project.

Questions To Ask / Checklist

I based my evaluation on a range of companies that I found either online or advertising in the writers' press at the time. However, this scene changes quickly, and in another 3-6 months' time there will be a different competitive line-up of companies with slightly different offers.

However, what an author NEEDS doesn't change very quickly. As technology progresses over the next few years, authors will look increasingly more to online solutions, but for the meantime, an author's needs are relatively static. So as long as you evaluate the services you are buying against the criteria below, you should get what you are paying for, irrespective of whether you are buying them item by item or from a publishing services company.

Critical assessment:

- do they offer an evaluation or critique service?

- o how much does this cost?
- o is it done by an experienced editor or book marketer?
- o can I see an example?
- o what authors have you worked on that I may have heard of?

Editing services:

- o spelling & grammar?
- o content and continuity?
- o include a marketing perspective?
- o proof-reading?
- o is a UK or US spell-checker used?

Jacket creation:

- o bespoke cover designs?
- o create artwork from templates?
- o artwork author's ideas?
- o do they require finished artwork?
- o who writes the jacket text?

Printing

- o short "digital" print runs
- o long "litho" print runs
- o print-on-demand
- o how do I obtain further copies? How much?
- o do they fund ongoing print runs?

Registrations

- o whose imprint?
- o who is the book registered with? In UK and/or US?

Distribution / wholesaling / fulfilment

- o UK or US distribution companies?
- o are book orders fulfilled from UK or US?
- o online or physical distributor?
- o what online companies listed with?
- o what shops listed with?
- o how do you promote to trade (bookshops) ?

Website

- o how do they promote their website?
- o do authors get given a webpage?

E-publishing

- o is it offered?

Credentials

- o what books have they produced that you may have heard of?
- o are the editors or publishers from any of the mainstream houses?

Print-on-demand: further questions

- o does the author get a digital version of the file?
- o if not, what happens when author ends his deal?
- o how can they reassure on consistency of quality?
- o where is the book printed?
- o do I have to ship to the UK from abroad?

If they supply Marketing / Promotional services, then check the following

Trade promotion:

- o do they write & issue AI sheets to distributors, wholesalers, libraries, booksellers?
- o do they have accounts with these companies?

Publicity services:

- o do they promote to the media?
- o do they have a database of contacts with whom you regularly liaise?
- o do they follow up all press releases issued?

Marketing services:

- o promote to the reader in any way?

TIME-LINE TO PUBLICATION: BEST PRACTICE

While writing your book	**Countdown to launch**
1. Read this book thoroughly, and other books that teach you about the publishing process contact my company for consultancy on self-publishing (via the *Indepublishing Consultancy website*).	Ideally 24 months in advance

2. Consider your options – whether you are:
   i Independently self-publishing
   ii Working with a self-publishing company
3. Learn how to self-publish
   i Map out what needs to be done to suit your particular genre of book
   ii Map out what you think you can do, and what you can't
   iii Do the maths – whether independently or partnering with a self-publishing services company.
4. Buy the *Writers' Handbook and Writers' Yearbook*
5. Subscribe to the book trade and writers' magazines
6. Join writers' and publishers' associations
7. Start a notebook with helpful names that might endorse, support and promote your book

If going completely solo:

8. Create your 'publisher' name, logo and stationery
9. Set up your business and visit your accountant
10. Register with Nielsen and Bowker
11. Start setting up accounts with distributor/wholesalers, and major book stores.

When manuscript is nearly complete	**Countdown to launch**
12. Verify all your facts (if non-fiction)	18 months
13. Check all copyrights and permissions	
14. Create bibliography, glossary, index and acknowledgements	
15. Source the right editor	
16. Source the right designer	
17. Consult your marketing / PR agent www.indepublishing.com is good startpoint	
18. Double-check your title isn't duplicated	
19. Buy domain name (if setting up a website; this is covered further in the sequel to this book)	
20. Start planning and source web developers	
21. Plan storage and fulfilment strategy	
Book production phase	
22. Edit to perfection	1 year
23. Design and artwork including back jacket text finalised	9 months
24. Set publication date	8 months
25. Get ISBN and barcode	7 months
26. Typeset	7 months
27. Proof read and sign off for print	6 months
28. Send AI sheet to your distributor in order to get into their monthly catalogues	6 months
29. Approve/amend printer-proof of book	5.5 months
During the printing phase	
30. Create your marketing and promotional plan	5 months
31. Prepare the AI sheet and database of relevant parties	5 months
32. Issue all AI sheets to book trade	4.5 months
33. Prepare mailing list database for publicity and reviews	4 months
34. Prepare range of relevant press releases aimed at the different audiences	4 months

(During the printing phase continued) — **Countdown to launch**

35. Plan and design promotional collateral ie. posters, flyers — 4 months
36. Book a clippings agency if you haven't got a PR company — 4 months
37. Start organising a book launch if you are hosting one — 4 months

Once review copies are received

38. Check them upon receipt – quantities, accuracy, quality etc — 4 months
39. Issue PR to media by email 4-2 months
40. Offer magazine articles to specialist magazines in your subject matter — 4-2 months
41. Issue Announcement Card to independent bookshops — 3 months
42. Chase PR emails; send out review copies to interested parties 2-0 months
43. distribute books to distributors, wholesalers, retail bookstores etc — 1 month

Launch

44. Launch event; PR it
45. Ideally organise a series of events over the next few months
46. Follow up with all media to see if they covered it

Post Launch

47. Review what worked and what didn't work; review clippings from the clippings agency; assess sales and where they were ie. How media & sales tied up.
48. Develop non-traditional avenues
49. Consider direct mail
50. Consider any spin-off ideas ie. Audio-tapes, ebooks, consulting etc.
51. Make a review / PR pack to show off successes to date and encourage bookshop stocks off the back of it

PART VII

MOVING FORWARD

CONCLUSIONS

It is evident that there are many, many routes to publication today, and that this has never been a better time to self-publish. What was once a closed shop now presents plenty of opportunity for the author. Authors can easily produce a high quality title that competes effectively in the marketplace; equally authors can choose to use their published book as a sales tool to attract the attentions of publishers and agents.

People happily read self-published titles when they don't know they are self-published

The nub of the question is whether the author has the right skills and knowledge to make a success of it. The essential work has to be good; get this endorsed by an independent editor or spokesperson before you waste precious pounds and many months of your time. Know what services you need to buy and which ones you can do to a high standard yourself.

Not all authors are good businessmen – in fact, many publishers would say that most authors would make poor businessmen. Equally, not all businessmen are writers. It is possible for one to learn the other's skill to a degree, but beyond that you will need to employ someone to do it well.

Know your own limitations – what you can do and what you have to buy in

Many authors focus on the print production element of the book as being the single biggest task, making the mistake of skipping through the groundwork of careful planning, overlooking the crafting work required on editing, proof-reading, design and simply not understanding the need to prepare timelines to launch.

Success is maximised by planning, crafting and preparing

The self-publisher's job is not necessarily to do everything, but to ensure that every task gets done. If you are going it alone, be clear about what you are getting for your money; at what point might the supplier start asking for additional budget if there are a number of revisions ie in design or editing.

If you are working with a self-publishing company, ensure both parties are clear about the quality of the final product and the ongoing relationship. Don't plan to 'cross bridges when you come to them', but ensure the agreement is watertight and crystal clear.

The self-publisher is the one who bears the greatest risk

Self-publishing is seen less and less as the 'book that got rejected'; instead, many self-published titles are seen as potential gems. Whilst publishing houses say that many of the manuscripts that come to them aren't good and that they are confident that potentially successful books will find their market, they also admit they miss some good manuscripts.. Don't take their rejection as the end of the road for your book. Whilst it is great to get your book accepted, thus endorsed, by a large publishing house, 'rejected' authors should not take rejection as their last opportunity.

"The lost chance is not the last chance"

(Leonid Sukhorukov)

History proves that many great authors were rejected and if it was not for their own self-belief and grim determination, we would not be reading many of our literary greats. The unspoken subtext to this is that maybe it was the rejection, and even continual rejection, that inspired their subsequent and greatest works to be written.

Inspiration and perfection are often due to bloody-minded determination

Get out there and work at it. THAT is how rejected authors have historically made it through the closed doors, and how they will continue to do so. Technology makes the process easier, but this self-same technology results in a plethora of books, thus making it harder for the real potential to be found.

Self-publishing maximises your chances of being found

This book proves that there are other avenues, depending on how much effort you are prepared to put in. If you are convinced that your writing is great, then prove it by getting an independent assessment from an editor (or five)… prove it by finding your audience. Endorsement is critical in publishing but it is difficult to get endorsement on an idea; publishing the book enables you to get endorsement of the product.

A self-published book is a sales tool – it is easier to market a product, not an idea

Self-publishing is critical when seeking to create a completely new concept. The author/publisher can put together the overall book package as he sees it, and this in itself may well be the catalyst to success.

Self-publishing is critical when creating a new concept

Obviously the ultimate arbiter of what's good and what's not is the potential reader. The complexity lies in getting your book in front of them. Rejections are made on a publisher's view of market potential and his view of market trends; mistakes get made and there's no point mentioning modern-day famous errors of judgement... after all, who was to say that a children's book of witchcraft & wizardry would become the catalyst to changing a generation of children's attitudes to reading?

The ultimate arbiter is the reader

Ultimately, financial prudence may tell you to spend your money on taking a holiday or building a conservatory rather than publishing your book – but it is your money and your choice. If you choose to publish your book, then throw yourself into it whole-heartedly, set yourself a financial ceiling and don't go above it.

Don't spend more than you can afford to

The advice is NOT that you shouldn't try. You should. You can't achieve great things if you don't try, and this sometimes means sticking your neck out even in the face of protests and warnings from friends and family. The advice IS to set a time limit on your publishing project. But be wise about it. Some actors, musicians, authors spend a lifetime chasing a dream, forgetting that life can offer other great opportunities. Don't get fixated on being a published author, and don't keep extending your deadline for success against loose promises.

Time has a value and it is irreplaceable. If your publishing project does not deliver a value in a set period of time, the stop, return to the day job and continue writing as a hobby. You can continue producing small numbers of copies of a self-published title for personal reasons, maybe sending them out as opportunities arise. But don't make yourself broke over your desire to be a published writer. There are no guarantees.

**Set a time limit;
if it doesn't deliver a value
then return to your day job**

Fictional books have a diffuse and elusive market consisting of general readers. They are difficult to find and sell to, and authors suddenly realise that publishing a book is easy in comparison to trying to sell it. Many self-publishing companies offer advice and will list your book on various databases, but none of these activities drive awareness of your book. Selling books is a whole new subject, but for the moment authors should reassure themselves that most books receive very little promotion. If you are prepared to throw yourself into the selling process, you can rest assured that your book will fall into the top 10% of promotional activity. As long as your activity is well targeted, it should result in sales.

**Producing a quality book is the first
step to selling your book**

A VISION FOR THE FUTURE

In the ideal world, we would have the richest possible choice and the ability to find it and buy it - niche titles mingling with mass-market, hot topics sitting cheek by jowl with fantastical tales and implausible theories.

But to achieve this Holy Grail, the industry needs to change considerably:

1. **There needs to be a greater acceptance of self-published books**
   a. Booksellers and book reviewers need to embrace 'the small man' more and give them a chance

2. **Self-publishing authors need to encourage this acceptance:**
   a. Authors have a responsibility to produce quality work
   b. Authors must take a more informed, business approach

3. **Companies offering self-publishing services need to co-ordinate in order to help independent authors:**
   a. Suppliers of services must consistently provide quality services
   b. Suppliers need to level the playing field by offering total clarity in advertising
   c. Standardisation in the description of self-publishing services to minimise any confusion

4. **We need to ensure the gems don't sit in slush piles, but empower authors to test the market themselves**

Also in this perfect world, every book will be beautifully produced with beautifully designed covers promising great revelations within; the work written to the highest standards with every word carefully chosen and every sentence beautifully structured. But this takes time and too few authors earn any real income out of writing. With a complex supply chain, extreme discounting, ease of download and copyright abuse, the demand for e-books to be cheap and book re-selling practices, authors see potential income from their hard work dwindle even further.

1. Authors need to earn a decent income from their work

2. Reinstate a value on the written word
    a. Discounting needs boundaries and guidelines

3. Set up guidelines and rules on discounting, reselling and copyrights to ensure authors receive a fair deal
    a. Buying use of text needs to be easier
    b. Authors should receive financial recompense when their text is accessed on the internet
    c. Review of how reselling works in order to protect author and publisher

Self-publishing has taken huge strides forward over the last few years. It now stands on the edge of a new future, and it is up to the self-publishing authors and companies to move it forward. It will either begin to happen, or not; but many believe that it has already started to happen.

ACKNOWLEDGEMENTS

Many people contributed to this book and made helpful comments to help shape opinions, expand knowledge and offer tips and advice for new authors. Without them, this book would be a lot thinner and have far less robust information.

The market is forever changing and it is tough to put a stake in the ground. I have learned a lot whilst writing it, and hope to keep learning.

I wish to thank everyone who gave up time to meet with me, take phone calls and exchange emails. Time is short in this life, and I appreciate the efforts made. I am also truly grateful for all the enthusiasm and positiveness I encountered along the way; there was no resistance but instead I was urged along with the words "*this book is desperately needed*." I hope the market receives it so positively.

I have tried very hard to reflect everyone's perspective and not to dilute anything as I transcribed their words from interview to written word. One of the biggest things I have learned is that if there are a million people involved in the publishing and bookselling industry, then there are a million opinions about what is right and wrong, what works and what doesn't, what should change and what shouldn't.

Some people will applaud statements made within, others may rant in objection. I cannot reflect everyone's opinion, but had to retain focus on 'what information will best help the new author get published'. This was the critical purpose for the book and all comments, statements, quotes and findings were selected purely on this basis. If I studied the publishing industry with a different question in mind, I am sure that other perspectives would have entered the frame.

THANK YOU TO:

Cover designs by Everyone
Artwork by Jacqueline Abromeit
Editing by Hilary Johnson
Typesetting by Linda Harris
Website by *www.cooltide.com*

Book trade
The Bookseller: *www.theBookseller.com*
The Booksellers Association: *www.booksellers.org.uk*
Publishing news: *www.publishingnews.co.uk*
Book Marketing Ltd: *www.bookmarketing.co.uk*
Booktrust: *www.booktrust.org.uk*
Society of Authors: *www.societyofauthors.net*
The Publishers Association: *www.publishers.org.uk*
The Independent Publishers Guild: *www.ipg.uk.com*
Derek Johns, President of AAA (Authors' Agents Association)
Jon Sievert, President of Bay Area Independent Publishers Assoc (US)
The Writer's Guild of GB: *www.writersguild.org.uk*
Nielsen BookData: *www.nielsenbookdata.com*
Bowker books in Print: *www.bowkerlink.com*
PubEasy: *www.pubeasy.com*
The British Library: *www.bl.co.uk*
Book Industry Communications: *www.bic.org.uk*
British Printing Industry Federation:
www.britishprint.com

Agents, publishers and booksellers
Penny Holroyde, Caroline Sheldon Literary Agents: 01983 760205
Andrew Franklin, Profile Books: *www.profilebooks.co.uk*
Michael Barnard, Macmillan: *www.macmillan.com*
Andrew Stilwell, Manager, London Review bookshop:
www.lrb.co.uk
Brian Finch, Maher Booksellers:
www.maherbooks.seekbooks.co.uk

Amazon: *www.amazon.co.uk*
Googleprint: *www.googleprint.com*
Abebooks: *www.abebooks.com*

Media

The Guardian journalists and editors include Robert McCrum, Literary Editor;Ashley Seager; John Ezard; DJ Taylor
The Telegraph
The Writer's Handbook

Authors

Louise Voss, author of *To be Someone; Are you my Mother; Lifesaver; Games People Play;*
Stephen Clarke, author of *A Year in the Merde; Merde Actually; Beam me U;, Who killed Beano?*
GP Taylor, author of *Shadowmancer; Wormwood; Tersias*
Preethi Nair, author of *Gypsy Masala, The Colour of Love; 100 Shades of White*
Gerald Howe, author of *Alfie's Adventures (the series)*
Deborah Lawrenson, author of *The Art of Falling*
Peter Murray, author of *Mokee Joe is Coming!; Mokee Joe Recharged; The Doomsday Trial*
George Courtauld, author of *The Pocket Book of Patriotism; A Pocket Book of Patriots*
John Morrison, author of *Anthony Blair, Captain of School: A Story of School Life by an Old Boy*
Jay Rayner, author of *The Marble Kiss*
Hillel Halkin, author of *A Strange Death; Across the Sabbath River and many translated books*
John F X Sundman, author of *Acts of the Apostles*
Elaine Boorish, author of *This Book is Unpublishable*

Full service self-publishing companies:

Able Publishing: *www.ablepublishing.co.uk*
Amherst Publishing: *www.amherstpublishing.co.uk*
Amolibros: *www.amolibros.com*
Ashridge Press: *www.country-books.co.uk*
Better Book Company: *www.better-book.co.uk*

The Book Guild: *www.bookguild.co.uk*
Matador: *www.troubador.co.uk*
Pen Press Publishers: *www.penpress.co.uk*

Print-on-demand publishers:
AuthorHouse: *www.authorhouse.co.uk*
AuthorsOnline: *www.authorsonline.co.uk*
Booksurge: *www.booksurge.com*
Diadem Books: *www.diadembooks.com*
Lulu: *www.lulu.com*
Planetree Publishing: *www.planetree-publishing.com*
Publish and be damned: *www.pabd.com*
Publish Britannica: *www.publishbritannica.com*
Trafford Publishing UK Ltd: *www.trafford.com*
UPSO : *www.upso.co.uk*
Writersservices: *www.writersservices.com*
Writersworld: *www.writersworld.co.uk*

Print on demand printers:
Antony Rowe: *www.antonyrowe.co.uk*
Lightning Source: *www.lightningsource.com*
RPM Print & Design: *www.rpm-repro.co.uk*
British Printing Industries Federation:
www.britishprint.com

Writing & Editing services
Hilary Johnson : *www.hilaryjohnson.demon.co.uk*
Publishers UK Ltd: *www.publishersukltd.co.uk*
Writing Ltd: *www.writing.co.uk*
The Writer's Workshop: *www.writersworkshop.co.uk*
Golgonooza: *www.nooza.com*
Society of Editors and Proofreaders: *www.sfep.org.uk*
Writers' services - *www.firstwriter.com*

Wholesalers/distributors:
Gardners: *www.gardners.com*
Bertrams: *www.bertrams.com*

THE END

Phew! I have written a whole book about publishing without once referring to J K Rowling.

RELEASING SPRING 2006

"What do I have to do to Sell a book!"

Whilst *"What do I have to do to get a book published!"* focussed purely on the production process of creating the best in order to make it desirable, its partner title *"What do I have to do to sell a book!"* is about communicating it to the right people.

Whilst I chose to address publishing first in this series of books, the fact is that marketing comes first. However, most authors that I have met always follow the same process - write, publish, market.

But marketing is not a bolt-on. It doesn't come at the end of the publishing process, but in fact at the very beginning. Every businessman starts off with a marketing plan, and it is no different for authors.

In the new order of self-publishing, author's write then pay someone to publish it for them rather than handing over any royalty percentages. At the point of receiving printed books, authors then choose whether to share out percentages by getting distribution and sales support. What self-publishing authors cannot do is then just cross their fingers and hope.

Many self-publishing authors have come a cropper in the past because what they didn't do before embarking on the whole self-publishing process is to PLAN. They didn't understand the process adequately, and they didn't research their market. Self-publishing authors would be well advised to take note of this important fact before embarking on many months of writing (which is time investment) and several thousand pounds of financial investment to publish and promote their book.

Selling books is hard, unrelenting work. Trying to find your audience is hard. Trying to convince your audience to buy is also hard. Days of effort can result in selling 2 or 3 books. For what profit? A few pounds? One pound?

There is no value in stock. It takes up space and deteriorates over time. The initial excitement of receiving boxes of books, freshly printed in their glossy covers, quickly turns to frustration as you keep heaving them from room to room as you try to reclaim ground that was once yours. Books that were so full of promise of returning an income can easily become valueless stock. Don't let this be the case. Don't just write and publish to a mantra of "I'm sure this will sell, I'm sure this will sell…" You need to know that it will sell, who to and how.

Marketing is a thorough process in itself, and most authors do not understand how to do a market analysis, how to write a marketing plan, how to place a value on a potential audience. But it is critical to learn.

Your book will only be found if you shout loud enough. Most authors believe that the world will be their oyster if they could only get the book into a large bookshop. It will sell if only people could see it. And yes, there is an element of truth in this. But your marketing plan has to amount to more than hoping a national buyer will stock the book in his chain of shops

Creating a book is MAGIC, marketing it is LOGIC… Marketing is a continual recycling of communication to audiences, building and growing. Sometimes your market is quickly saturated. Other times the market is too small to warrant further production. On occasion, it is immensely successful. The magic is in the vision to produce something that everybody wants. The logic is in communicating its presence.

The product (your book) has to be good. What publishing and marketing cannot do is sell something that people don't want or aren't ready for. Your first book launch is the most expensive, in terms of time and financial investment.

Doing 'something different'. There is obviously huge merit in being different and unique; however it is critical to be different for a reason, not just to be different. Consumers are bombarded with new products every day and are sophisticated in determining a product's value – will it do what it says on the tin? Or am I just being sold a marketing ploy? Nobody wants to feel the fool and will quickly see through a ploy. Think carefully about the benefit of the book's point of difference.

Remain realistic and grounded. Self-publishing authors have to have a lot of self-belief in order to wade their way through the publishing minefield and bookselling battleground. If you're thin-skinned, lazy or lack self-motivation, then stop here and save yourself the hard work.

It is said that authors who have a publishing contract with a mainstream house often have unrealistic expectations about what a publishing house can do for them, in terms of the amount of time dedicated to individual titles. Some authors still sit back and let the process happen around them, maybe even baulking at self-promotion. Some authors want to participate but don't know how. This book will also benefit this type of author, and your publishing house will undoubtedly be eternally grateful for all the effort you are prepared to put. Just a word of advice... work *with* them. Always keep them informed of what you are planning to do and exploit the opportunity of having their expertise to support your efforts.

So? Should you not bother?

Having been so negative about an author's chances of success, there is good news. This is that you can undertake any initial investigative work whilst still holding down a good, paying job…

- Research and plan before jacking in the job and hiding yourself in the country to write.
- Listen and learn before investing time, effort and money into a publishing venture.
- Do some initial investigative work to find a potential value in your marketplace, and better understand what you are writing and why you are writing it.
- Once you can articulate precisely what you are writing and you can see how to reach that audience, then you are ready to begin the publishing process.

But all of this, you know. I can hear you turning the pages saying *yes, yes, yes, I know all this; I just don't know how to drive that awareness and demand. What is marketing? Just give me some answers!*

Marketing is communicating...
the RIGHT information
to the RIGHT people
in the RIGHT place
at the RIGHT time
...repeatedly

That's the answer in a nutshell. Do your homework. Read the book. The self-publishing author must be responsible for the marketing as he has the most to gain or lose.